WILLIAM S. BURROUGHS'
"THE REVISED BOY SCOUT MANUAL"

# WILLIAM S. BURROUGHS'
# "THE REVISED BOY SCOUT MANUAL"

## AN ELECTRONIC REVOLUTION

## WILLIAM S. BURROUGHS

Edited and with prefaces by
Geoffrey D. Smith & John M. Bennett

With a foreword by Antonio Bonome
and
an afterword by V. Vale

THE OHIO STATE UNIVERSITY PRESS
COLUMBUS

Library of Congress Cataloging-in-Publication Data
Names: Burroughs, William S., 1914–1997, author. | Smith, Geoffrey D. (Geoffrey Dayton), 1948– editor. | Bennett, John M., editor. | Bonome, Antonio, writer of foreword. | Vale, V., writer of afterword.
Title: William S. Burroughs' "The Revised Boy Scout Manual" : an electronic revolution / edited and with prefaces by Geoffrey D. Smith & John M. Bennett ; with a foreword by Antonio Bonome and an afterword by V. Vale.
Other titles: Revised Boy Scout Manual
Description: Columbus : The Ohio State University Press, [2018] | "Bulletin 23." | Includes bibliographical references.
Identifiers: LCCN 2018013635 | ISBN 9780814254899 (pbk. ; alk. paper) | ISBN 0814254896 (pbk. ; alk. paper)
Subjects: LCSH: Burroughs, William S., 1914–1997. Revised Boy Scout Manual. | Burroughs, William S., 1914–1997—Criticism and interpretation.
Classification: LCC PS3552.U75 R48 2018 | DDC 813/.54—dc23
LC record available at https://lccn.loc.gov/2018013635

Cover design by Andrew Brozyna
Text design by Juliet Williams
Type set in Adobe Sabon and Trade Gothic
Published by The Ohio State University Press

# CONTENTS

# ACKNOWLEDGMENTS

We extend our sincere gratitude to all the people who helped with this project, without whom it would never have come to fruition:

James Grauerholz, Executor of the William S. Burroughs Estate;

Isaac Gewirtz, Curator of the Henry W. and Albert A. Berg Collection of English and American Literature at the New York Public Library;

Rob Spindler, University Archivist and Head, Archives and Special Collections, Arizona State University Libraries;

Lisa Iacobellis, Program Coordinator / Special Collections, The Ohio State University; and

Rebecca Jewett, Coordinator of Public Services & Operations, Thompson Special Collections.

# FOREWORD

Antonio Bonome

## 3. PREAMBLE: "ET LA CHAIRE S'EST FAITE VERBE . . . ET PUIS, À PEINE UNE LUMIÈRE"

In the beginning was the Word, and the Word was God—
and the word was flesh human flesh . . . in the beginning
of writing.[1]

New York, 1939. William S. Burroughs severs the distal phalanx of his left little finger with the purpose of impressing someone named Jack Anderson.[2]

Tangier, 1954. Letter to Ginsberg: He has sent Allen the story that describes the 1939 episode so that he may find a publisher for the text.

London, 1969. Burroughs finishes *The Wild Boys*, where Jack Anderson has now morphed into one mysterious figure from a parallel dimension called John Hamlin. No news from the finger.

## 2. AMBLE: "THAT DANGEROUS SUPPLEMENT"

Every phrase, in Burroughs' view, has a similarly check-
ered history of incarnations and migrations. The production of the cut-up text thus raises the question of
who is speaking in a given phrase or fragment. Like the
deconstructionists, the writer of cut-ups implies that it is
always language that speaks within a network of infinite
and anonymous citations.[3]

Patients suffering from "body integrity identity disorder"
(BIID) complain that a particular limb does not belong
to them, and consequently demand the "surplus" healthy
appendage amputated.[4] This desire to amputate the *parasite*
organ seems to be symmetrically opposed to the perception
of a "phantom limb" in people that have suffered the invol-
untary amputation of an extremity.[5]

In more than one metaphorical way, *The Revised Boy
Scout Manual* negotiates its existence between the phan-
tasmatic and the parasitic. Until recently, this book clearly
marked an absence, an aural blind spot between *Entretiens
avec William Burroughs* (1969), later published in English
as *The Job* (1970), and *The Electronic Revolution* (1970).
It was a phantom text, something "extra," that haunted the
archival vault: the document of a disembodied voice recorded
in three cassettes dated in 1970.

Perhaps some readers familiar with *The Job* and *The
Electronic Revolution* will ask after reading the *RBSM*[6]
how big a quote can be, and which text is quoting which,
a perfectly reasonable and much-needed interrogation. They
might even feel compelled to ask for the amputation of the
surplus text. Two unusual and perhaps uncomfortable vectors might lie behind this urge or conflict.

On the one hand, these two works fold into the puzzling
audio text, producing a clear, concise portrait of Burroughs'
working process during those years. Textually, the result-

ing multimodal combination unsettles the borders of the
"book" concept, precluding the possibility of any final draft.
In spite of their existence as three separate objects, their closure remains undecided. On the other hand, such a conclusion is possible only if we simultaneously defer and accept
the fact that Burroughs often worked in series. The most
palpable example is *The Nova Trilogy*, which consists of
three different selections and rearrangements from roughly
the same manuscript with three different titles. On the next
level, almost as in an infinite regression, *The Soft Machine*
idea of displaying the same title for (at least) two different
novels, corresponding to the first and second editions.[7] More
importantly, and quoting again Robin Lyndenberg, "Like
the deconstructionists, the writer of cut-ups implies that it is
always language that speaks within a network of infinite and
anonymous citations" (loc. cit.). Thus, the fact that closure
is postponed seems like an invitation by Burroughs to reflect
about language, perhaps in terms similar to Lyndenberg's
statement, but above all to succumb to the urge and engage
in the cut-up game.

Let us add some fuel to the fire: the underground publishing company RE/Search printed a transcript fraction of
the first tape of the original recording in 1982, illustrated
with photographs by Charles Gatewood, collages, and drawings (one of them by legendary artist Paul Mavrides), which
only made the *RBSM* the more enigmatic, giving the aforementioned fraction a "seemingly" autonomous life of its
own. Only seemingly, since the original "extra," now disjointed and transposed to a different medium, was combined
with more extras of different species and supplemented with
more writings by Burroughs and Brion Gysin, and interviews
with Throbbing Gristle and Genesis P-Orridge. Thanks to
the textual and sociological synchronic context, that fraction
was a different text.

The RE/Search piece shows how a project sparked by
Burroughs and Gysin's collaboration had transformed the
context of its reception, disseminated by the underground

press through infection, fracture, and semiotic recombination. It also is an *amputation* of the original manuscript, and there are two interesting absences in it: the first absence comes from the lack of the other two tapes' transcripts, while the second is felt in the elusiveness of the mother lode, a second word hoard in Burroughs' production *The Wild Boys*. More importantly, the fanzine also shows a remarkable embodiment process; Burroughs' writing was producing semiotic and gender activists in the flesh, that is, some artists who could be ascribed to the industrial scene. Conversely, the men in the flesh who modeled (like those of a painter) for the characters in the *The Wild Boys*,[8] will evolve in Burroughs' further writings into "bodies of light;"[9] they become text and specter like the 1939 finger.

So far, this foreword has underlined the feedback relation between text, body, and action that occurred in a certain context, that is, the eighties, as far as Burroughs' experimental production is concerned. Just consider the current state of affairs, and use the Burroughsian lens that you are holding now: see that monster there, waiting?

## 1. POSTAMBLE: "I WAS WAITING THERE IN SOMEONE ELSE'S WRITING"

The phasmid—the mythic animal of the anti-Platonist, as you will see—acquires its power from the following paradox: by realizing a kind of imitative perfection, it shatters the hierarchy that can be demanded of all imitation. There are no longer a model and its copy: there's a copy that has devoured its model, and the model no longer exists, while the copy alone, by a strange law of nature, enjoys the privilege of existing. The imitated model thus becomes an accident of its copy—a fragile accident in danger of being engulfed—and no longer the other way around. Less-than-being has eaten being, possessed being, *it is* in its place. (Or, to the contrary, couldn't one say that what we have here is the mythic animal of the Platonist, for whom the model that is truly adopted, *digested,* would provide the most perfect illustration of the power of the idea? But let us move on.)[*sic*][10]

Phasmid comes from the Greek "φάσμα" (phasma), which stands for apparition, specter, or screen image. Today the word *phasmid* refers to three different objects:

1. A sensory structure in nematodes, which are unicellular worms, many of them parasites.
2. A mimetic stick-bug. This is the animal Georges Didi-Huberman writes about in the quote above.
3. A type of hybrid-cloning vector used in biotechnology.

The concept "replication" is present in three contemporary senses of the word, where also resonate the spectral, the viral, the parasitic, the clonic, all of them related to the notion "survival." The *RBSM* is a handbook for the postmodern code and gender warrior's continued existence. It traces some strategies used by repressive forces that can be reversed, and proposes some drills for survival that lean heavily on replication. Burroughs was undoubtedly a prospective writer: text and body go together in his work, and both are multiple, serial, necessarily monstrous in their being in a time that is out of joint. He is prescient of the discursive character of both: no degree zero is possible since both are open to parasitism since the outset, and both must be finally performed through contamination and heterogeny.

From 1967 onward, Burroughs will be busy with the story of a portmanteau ghost that is himself, only younger. Audrey Carsons will be patterned after (among other sources) his perception of Denton Welch, and after Richard Blum's story "The House by the Water."[11] Burroughs was "waiting there in their writing," and there is almost certainly in Audrey a good portion of that Boy Scout in Los Alamos that once he was. Through writing he will propel himself into his work, as a teenage phantom, becoming writing and, eventually, a ghost in a screen.

A final act of disappearance that can perfectly stand alongside those acts performed by The Great Thurston, that incredible magician from Columbus, Ohio.

## 1. ENTER WARGAME

# BRIEF TEXTUAL HISTORY

Geoffrey D. Smith

Homer's epics were performance art, recited orally and augmented, historicized and localized over generations. Several thousand years later, William S. Burroughs became a practitioner of twentieth-century performance art, utilizing new media and technology to enliven his literary activities. So too, like Homer's, his original work, transcribed by editors and translators, assumed an autonomy of representation that, although remaining essentially Burroughs, in basic content, attained distinct textual states through accretion, nuance, and disintegration. A case in point is the work at hand, originally *The Revised Boy Scout Manual,* now *"The Revised Boy Scout Manual": An Electronic Revolution* (*RBSM*), which, in its totality, exists in typescripts, tape recordings, periodical publications, books, and online. Significant differences occur throughout the textual history: subtle but accumulative substantive changes, major portions lacking from one source but appearing in another, inchoate passages disappearing entirely from any published state. The work then changes over time with each rendition credible in its own right. (Of particular note, as I will explain further below, is that the principal source text for the *RBSM* is the

W. S. BURROUGHS: *THE REVISED BOY SCOUT MANUAL*. READ BY WSB.
COPIED BY VALE FROM CASSETTES SUPPLIED BY GENESIS P-ORRIDGE.

tape-recorded version, thus reverting to an oral tradition.)
Such a textual history is not unique—conspicuously, the multiple versions of Walt Whitman's *Leaves of Grass* come to
mind—but that fact does not assuage the textual challenges
for completing a single edited work that will prove useful to
both the Burroughs reader and the Burroughs scholar.

## TEXTUAL NOTES

The role of textual editors in scholarly and bibliographic
research is to identify, collate, and reconcile various versions
of a literary text in order to approach an ideal text. Such
is the undertaking for *The Revised Boy Scout Manual* by
William S. Burroughs. An author, especially a literary inno-
vator such as Burroughs, can be resistant to the concept of
an authoritative or stable text, but an authoritative textual

edition is not meant to concretize the literary work; rather, through interactive amalgamation of multiple versions, it aims to illuminate both the congruent and variant editorial decisions in order to perpetuate and sustain a vibrant text. The first step in textual editing, traditional yet still useful, even mandatory, is selection of the copy-text, a working text from which variants of other texts radiate and can be documented in notes and appendices while the edited working text remains an unmarked, reading copy.

In the case of *RBSM,* the earliest source is Burroughs' typescript copy, with authorial annotations held in the Berg Collection of the New York Public Library (NYPLTS 1). The Berg copy, however, contains only thirty-six pages of the full typescript. Arizona State University Library holds a photocopy of the near-complete original Burroughs typescript (it lacks page 31), also with authorial annotations (AZTS 1). Most of the emendations for both NYPLTS 1 and AZTS 1 are the same text, in Burroughs hand, but not identical; that is, the AZTS 1 photocopy is not a photocopy of the emended NYPLTS 1 since, though many changes are the same, handwriting discrepancies confirm that they were done separately. One can only speculate: Burroughs may have been working with both the original typescript and photocopy at the same time, making changes to each as he held them side by side; or he may have worked on one first, then another at a later time. Because NYPLTS 1 has additional changes not part of AZTS 1, it would suggest that Burroughs made the simultaneous changes, transmitted AZTS 1 to another party, kept NYPLTS 1 as his working copy, and made subsequent changes that were not added to AZTS 1.

As sound as these typescripts would prove as copy-texts, the most essential source is the set of audiotapes of Burroughs' reading of *RBSM.* Reverting to the oral tradition, of performance art, Burroughs' reading not only incorporates substantive changes to the text from which he is reading but also adds the dimension of tone and emphasis, which are not evident in the typescripts. Again, one must speculate, but the tape does pick up the sound of rustling papers as Burroughs reads; the exactness of the reading to the typescripts, with its aforementioned extemporaneous alterations, strongly suggests that he was reading from the complete, unedited NYPLTS 1 since changes to that document are not heard in the reading. Throughout the reading (very consistently at the beginning, sporadic in later portions), Burroughs makes direct statements about structure and punctuation (e.g., "new paragraph"; "period"; "dash"; etc.), implying that his reading was intended for transcription.

Another resource is the Vale version of *RBSM,* a small part of which was published in *RE/Search #4/5* (San Francisco, 1982). The Vale version was apparently typeset from listening to the audiotapes, as the same extemporaneous changes made by Burroughs in his reading and noted by the editors appear in the Vale text. It is also apparent that Vale did not have access to the typescripts since later authorial emendations are not noted. Although the Vale version would seem to be a redundant text, it serves two general purposes: affirmation of the editors' transcription of the tape and clarification of difficult passages due to either poor technical rendition or less-than-clear reading by Burroughs on the tape. On the latter point, during the taping session, Burroughs began slowly and precisely, but as he entered deeper into the text, his pace, although never rapid, did speed up, and elisions, dialect, accent, and his performance mode render many readings ambiguous. (Burroughs' performance readings, however, enliven the narrative, for example, the English accent of the major domo in the Claridge raid or the German accent of Herr Doktor Kurt von Steinplatz.) Vale essentially provided a separate set of ears for transcribing these difficult passages.

A final substantive resource is *The Electronic Revolution* (Expanded Media Editions, West Germany, 1970; rpt. Cambridge, England, 1971) an interpolated version of *RBSM* that has extensive added passages that are lacking in other versions but included in the volume at hand.

Still other documents are included in appendices. Principally, a second typescript from the New York Public Library, NYPLTS 2, is an inchoate version of *RBSM*. The primary themes are evident and some passages almost identical to those in later versions, but it is clearly an early effusion, rough and hurried, that Burroughs would later structure and craft into what became *RBSM*. NYPLTS 2 is the ur-text for *RSM* and is transcribed exactly for an appendix (i.e., line endings, strike-throughs, obvious misspellings, etc., are recorded exactly as they appear in NYPLTS 2). The AZTS 1 also includes typescript fragments that do not appear in any other version, and they too, like NYPLTS 2, are transcribed exactly and included in an appendix. The final appendix, "The Feedback from Watergate to the Garden of Eden," precedes *The Electronic Revolution* in the Expanded Media Editions; and, though it has tenuous correlation to *RBSM*, it is seen as an important corollary document in the assessment of *RBSM* because of its integral, textual positioning and related themes. The final text of *RBSM* is an amalgamation of the five source texts (NYPLTS 1, NYPLTS 2, AZTS 1, Vale, *The Electronic Revolution*) as measured against the audiotapes of Burroughs' reading, presumably, from NYPLTS 1. The final text is a fair text, without evidence of editorial intervention, and largely reproduces NYPLTS 1 and AZTS 1. Variant readings are recorded in the notes section so that any reader can reconstruct any version of *RBSM*. The notes also include annotations and, in some cases, the rationale for selection of variant readings.

Just as Homer's epic evolved through centuries of the oral transmission of texts, Burroughs' writings (and all texts) have evolved and will continue to evolve as well, though with the advent of the Internet, versions will proliferate at an unimagined pace. Individuals post texts on the Internet with seeming impunity, despite copyright law, and corruptions and alterations (both unintended and intended) can and do occur. With the nearly instant dissemination of texts, such suspect versions of literary works subvert and confuse the choice of reliable texts and, subsequently, literary hermeneutics. Though the editors do not claim the current edition of *RBSM* to be definitive, we do claim it as a reliable scholarly text, a single resource that provides not only a fair text for the general reader but also a research resource for Burroughs specialists.

## SILENT EMENDATIONS

Because the source documents use both English spellings (NYPLTS 1, AZTS 1, *The Electronic Revolution*) and American spellings (Vale), the editors chose to regularize the text to American spellings on the assumption that Burroughs is ultimately an American author. Punctuation is regularized to the copy-text (NYPLTS 1 and AZTS 1) since textual theory proffers that an author's earliest manuscripts are truer to his intrinsic punctuation patterns, that is, accidentals. Obvious misspellings are silently emended while idiosyncratic ones are retained, but apparent grammatical errors, if corrected, are recorded in the notes. Abbreviations and sources precede the notes at the end of the book.

# DID BURROUGHS HAVE A PLAN?

John M. Bennett

It is hard not to read this text, legendary but fragmentary in numerous underground and avant-garde circles, and wonder about the author's intentions. One asks questions: Is this a serious manual for destabilizing the State? Is it black comedy? Is it a social mirror, revealing—perhaps indirectly—the world we live in? Without attempting to answer these questions (in truth, the answer to *all* of them is, to some extent, yes), I think we can identify some textual and stylistic aspects to this work and its various sections that may help lead the reader to some conclusions. It should be noted that this process could lead to a broader understanding of Burroughs' work as a whole, since almost all the themes, topics, and "routines" (to use his own term) in *The Revised Boy Scout Manual* appear again and again throughout his work, in which it is helpful to think of Burroughs' voice as speaking through a constantly shifting set of masks or personae, sometimes changing them in the same sentence.

There are at least eight kinds of writing in *The Revised Boy Scout Manual* to consider in this light:

1. Historical and social analysis, as in the book's opening paragraphs;

2. Conjecture about possible alternative sociohistorical scenarios, as on pages 4–5, with the author's speculations about an alternative course of action that Bolívar might have followed;

3. Technical advice and information on weaponry and tactics, as beginning on page 6;

4. Fantasy scenarios of actions and events, stemming from WSB's interest in science fiction, and from his "Routines," a form he used in various permutations throughout his work; an extensive example of this begins on page 12 with the ERP—English Republican Party—a front for subversive and theatrical activities against the Queen and the social order;

5. Discussion of the use of language, cut-up techniques, and "scrambling" to affect social reality and consciousness (related to no. 3 above), as starting on page 42;

6. Citations of research into mental functioning, memory, drugs, and the like, to bolster his proposals for social action;

7. Clear-headed assessments of the effectiveness and morality of the methods and scenarios he discusses, as in the book's very last paragraphs in which he speaks of this work as a "utopian fantasy";

8. Nostalgia for a boyhood in an idealized Midwestern setting.

With respect to no. 1, the book opens with a passage in which WSB seems to wish to establish an objective and serious framework for his proposals. This serves as a way to segue into a mode of "what if" speculation (no. 2), giving his speculation a greater air of plausibility: for example, what if Bolívar had promoted Chinese immigration? This is not as far-fetched as it might seem, as throughout the 16th through

19th centuries, various attempts were made to control social development in Latin America through selective immigration policies. With the first section of technical advice (no. 3), WSB makes his first subtle shift into a science-fiction-like fantasy, although the equipment and methods he proposes are not at all outrageously unrealistic. In fact, many of them had, or have by now been, put into practice by revolutionaries, activists, and terrorists worldwide.

By the time he gets to the "schema" (page 12) for the United Kingdom, he moves into seriocomedic fantasies (no. 4), and the writing style changes from fairly straightforward expository prose to something much more dramatic, with shouts of "Bugger the Queen!" and a plethora of voices and dialogue from a variety of characters, named and unnamed. One of his characters even uses a comic German accent and diction. These are the passages (some of the liveliest and most entertaining in the book) that suggest a black humor and a paradoxical pleasure in the satiric playing out of some of the consequences of the more serious ideas he presents elsewhere in the book. It's as if he wishes that those ideas could be put into practice but realizes that they are largely impractical.

Some of the most interesting passages of the book from an ideational point of view are those (no. 5) in which he discusses the use of language cut-ups as a means to affect the course of events. This, of course, is territory that was especially interesting to WSB as a writer, since he employed such techniques extensively in his own writing and with audiotape and film. The use of these techniques as a way to change consciousness is an idea he took quite seriously, and applying them to the social and cultural realm, as he does in this book, creates one of the most compelling parts of the work. It's something he seems to think could actually work, and thus there is little sarcasm, and more autobiography, in such passages, as, for example, the one beginning on page 42.

Almost equally serious are his citations and discussions of experimental psychology and the use of drugs to change social reality (no. 6).

Whatever WSB's intentions, it is perhaps ironic that many of the techniques, processes, and scenarios he presents have come to pass since 1970, when he was working on this Manual, in the hands of both state and external actors, in the form of terrorist actions, state surveillance, social movements of all political stripes, and so on. Again, whatever WSB's intentions, this book can be read as a prescient warning of things that came to be, and that will come to be in the future. He seems to satirize extremes of all kinds, but *at the same time* to see them as a not-unreasonable pathway to social change.

At the root of that change is another constant throughout WSB's work, present in this one as well: no. 8, his nostalgia for a partly idealized boyhood in the American Midwest, as on pages 8–9, when he rhapsodizes about the "freshwater panfish . . . of . . . Missouri and Arkansas . . . ," or in his description of regions of Ecuador as similar to the "Ozark mountains," or the coastal areas where "redbrick cities" could be built (pages 33–34). This view of the Americas as an earthly paradise, here mixed with WSB's nostalgic reminiscences of his childhood, has been resonating in the Eurocentric mind since 1492.

Perhaps it is this nostalgia for a lost world—and an anger at the dysfunctionality and ugliness of the world WSB sees around him—that forms the core dynamic of this book and of much of his other work. This dynamic, and the ambiguities and paradoxes it engenders, are what make him an endlessly complex, thought-provoking, and fascinating artist. In the end, however, he can see things coldly and clearly, as in this book's conclusion, or "END OF THE WAR GAME," in which he talks about some of the techniques he describes as "utopian fantasy" and points out that they could well be counterproductive (no. 7). He concludes by apparently affirming a belief in the effectiveness of the ". . . weapons that change consciousness—cut-ups, scrambling, use of videotapes, etc. The weapons of illusion." Perhaps through illusion we will find a way? A hope in illusion seems fundamentally ambiguous—things could change, but would the change be "real"? If there is anything that characterizes Burroughs' work as whole, it is perhaps this very ambiguity: ambiguity of intention, of humor vs. bitterness, of affirmation vs. denial, of analysis vs. paranoia, of love vs. fear, and of persistent memory vs. memory's suppression.

# "THE REVISED BOY SCOUT MANUAL"

## AN ELECTRONIC REVOLUTION[1]

BE PREPARED
"Zur jeden massen Mord stehen wir bereit"
For every mass murder let us stand PREPARED
(Old S. A. song)[2]

NOTHING IS TRUE. EVERYTHING IS PERMITTED.

LAST WORDS OF HASSAN I SABBAH THE OLD MAN OF
THE MOUNTAIN[3]

## THE REVISED BOY SCOUT MANUAL
## BULLETIN 23
## REVOLUTIONARY WEAPONS AND TACTICS

Since World War I revolutionary weapons and tactics have undergone a biologic mutation to survive the invention of heavy weapons. Anyone can make a sword, a spear, a bow-and-arrow in his basement or spare-room workshop. He can make some approximation of a small arm. He cannot make automatic weapons, tanks, bombers, fighter-planes, destroyers, artillery. These heavy weapons are in the hands of reactionary forces, which gives them an overwhelming advantage in direct combat. With heavy weapons five percent of the population can hold down 95 percent by sheer force. This advantage, which did not exist before heavy weapons, must now be taken into account. (A belated development to be sure. The stupidity of the military mind is unbelievable. Towards the end of the Civil War in the States a crude machine gun and a crude tank were rejected by President Lincoln's military advisors as impractical. Now these weapons were primitive to be sure, but quite usable, and all the elements were there. In World War II General Gamelin[4] thought that tanks were unimportant—until they poured around the end of his Maginot line. General Gamelin did not like tanks.) So plinking around the streets with a Beretta 25 is little to the purpose and still less a Colt Army 45 hand gun so inaccurate it is more dangerous to friend than enemy, your friends being closer to it. It is a very myopic hand gun. Bombs in the Post Office, in the police stations? What is this, the I. R. A. in 1916?[5] Blow up the Statue of Liberty would you? Have you any idea how much good gelignite it would take to explode that old beast? The same explosive material discreetly placed could bring down the economic system of the West. The Scout Manual will show you how.

The extent to which revolutionary theory and tactics is disadvantageously shaped by opposition is something few revolutionaries like to think about, being for the most part as bigoted and impervious to facts as those whom they think they oppose. In 1848[6] a world-wide liberal movement was ruthlessly crushed in Europe and vitiated in South America. Consider how present-day revolutionaries are being Cheguevera'd back into the 19th century to repeat the mistakes of Garibaldi and Bolivar.[7] Bolivar liberated a large section of South America from Spain. He left intact the Christian calendar, the Spanish language, the Catholic church, the Spanish bureaucracy. He left Spanish families holding the wealth and land. He must have loved the conquistadores in some corner of his being, to treat them with such exemplary consideration. It is a familiar pattern. The oppressed love the oppressors and cannot wait to follow their example. Morocco, independent from France, takes over the inefficient French bureaucracy. Arab countries liberated from England retain the barbarous English method of execution. Cannot a revolution make a clean sweep of all this old garbage? To achieve independence from alien domination and to consolidate revolutionary gains, five steps are necessary:

1. Proclaim a new era and set up a new calendar;
2. Replace alien language;
3. Destroy or neutralize alien Gods;
4. Destroy alien machinery of governmental control;
5. Take wealth and land from individual aliens.

Suppose that Bolivar had followed this program:
1. He sets up a new calendar with no reference to A.D., B.C. No Saint Days, no Christian Holidays, no more Semanas Santas.
2. There are 35 mutually incomprehensible Indian dialects in Peru alone. South America constitutes a tower of Babel. Unifying language is essential, but not the colonial languages Spanish and Portuguese. Bolivar decides that the language in South America will be Chinese. Several considerations dictate this choice. He has been impressed by the

equanimity of the Chinese, their quiet self-possession in the dreariest and most forbidding places. Here is a town in the high Andes—a gloomy, windy pass. Thin air like death in the throat, from the low, sod huts with no chimneys the sullen bestial inhabitants peer out, eyes red with smoke. No trees, wind-swept grass, little terraced fields above which the mountains tower to stone and snow. The proprietor of the one general store is an old Chinese; he has been there many years, you can tell. Unhurried and old he fills an order for provisions. All places are alike to him. This quiet possession of his own space can only be attributed to the structure of the Chinese language. There are also aesthetic considerations. A river town in coastal Ecuador—malarial faces like dirty grey paper. Down the mud street steps a girl, naked to the waist, black as ebony, with fine mongoloid features and straight hair. Negro and Chinese. ZOWIE. Then, Chinese characters look better on signs or on the printed page. His main consideration is to build up the economy by attracting the frugal and industrious Chinese settlers. Chinese will be taught in all schools. Place and street names will be Chinese.

3. It is not necessary to track whiskey priests through the brush. Lands and property of the church confiscated, no religious instruction in schools—simply make it disadvantageous and uninteresting to be a Catholic.

4. The Spanish bureaucracy, which starts with one incompetent, lazy, dishonest, superfluous bastard, who then fills an office with all his incompetent relatives, all filling out senseless forms, must be attacked at its roots. All forms and records to be destroyed.

5. Land and property of resident Spaniards confiscated. Those who choose to remain must integrate into the working community. The children will not speak Spanish or kneel in any Christian church. So the face of history is changed.

To return from this illustrated fantasy, consider the weapons and tactics available to present-day revolutionaries in the West.

Small arms and similar weapons

Most useful all-around hand gun is the pig 38 special. Anyone with reasonable coordination can be taught in 12 rounds to hit a foot-square target at 30 feet, and that's practical pistol shooting. The lightweight models with two-inch barrel are quite accurate, which makes this gun one of the lightest and most compact of all powerful hand guns.

Hand guns can be traced. Possession is a crime and serves as provocation.

Home-made weapons are useful and every good scout will be tinkering with cross-bows and rubber-band guns, home-made flame throwers and laser guns, cyanide injectors and blow guns. Match-lock and flint-lock pistols shooting a load of crushed glass and cyanide crystals are quite effective at six feet. The simplest cyanide injector has a large plunger that can be grasped in the whole hand—you shove the needle in and push plunger home in the same thrust. A more sophisticated model looks like a toy pistol. Needle is unscrewed from end of barrel; the pistol cocked by drawing back spring attached to plunger; a sponge soaked in cyanide solution is inserted in the barrel, and needle and cap screwed back into place; when trigger releases the spring a massive dose of cyanide solution is squeezed into the flesh, causing instant death. When not in use needle is capped by a Buck Rogers death ray. If you can catch the target with mouth open you can jet it in from 10 feet like a spitting cobra. This is not hard to do. They are always ranting on about permissiveness, marihuana, anarchy, ill-bred attacks on her majesty; bring back hanging, bring back flogging, heavier penalties for drug offenses; ban smut, etc. And of course the injector is at home in bars and restaurants. Instead of canarde à l'orànge,[8] he gets a mouthful of prussic acid. A bolo made from a bicycle chain with lead weights at each end; knives with a blade that flies off, propelled by a powder charge or a powerful spring in the handle; and vibrating knives with a vibrator in the handle. A double-edged knife on a spring that can be whipped back and forth. Ingenuity will turn up many novel designs: cross-bows, rubber-band guns powered by a powerful rubber band can shoot a lead slug with considerable force and accuracy up to 20 yards, long-range blow guns, etc. These weapons are useful for individual assassination.

Assassination by list

So who do you assassinate by list? Not the obvious targets—the politicians, narks, and pigs. They are servants who obey orders—so the targets are not the front man, but the higher-ups behind the scenes. You announce that you have a list of these secret controllers and that they will be killed one after the other. The list is guess work of course, but the real higher-ups will soon expose themselves. So for a start we assassinate a Swiss banker—never go wrong on that. Just get a list of high Swiss bankers and pull his name out of a hat. This is assassination by rist—ABL. The rich and powerful cower behind guards and electric fences.

Random Assassination (RA)

The ingenious concept of random assassination has been proposed by Brion Gysin.[9] Five people a day in five districts of a city are killed. Category of person and district are determined by lot. One way would be to shuffle a pack of cards listing various categories—housewife, bowler hat and umbrella, nun, meth drinker, lavatory attendant, anyone driving or riding in a Bentley, etc. Then shuffle another pack of city areas arranged into districts that do not correspond to the actual boroughs or wards. Since the choice is completely random there is no pattern and the assassinations cannot be predicted or anticipated. Exempt from this daily lottery are the police and the military. The reason they are accorded this position of privilege: to stir resentment in the populace and so set the stage for a subsequent accusation that Rightist plotters carried out RA to create an emergency and seize power. RA applied to group units could paralyze the economy of the West, and this brings us to

Bombs and explosive devices

Post Offices, public buildings, and monuments are quite useless targets in most cases. With less risk and less outlay of material you could paralyze the whole communications system, like this: Two Israeli passenger planes recently exploded, probably as a result of bombs planted in freight or luggage by terrorists. Already these lines are banned and nobody will fly on the planes. Now suppose you plant five bombs a day at random, how long before no one flies or ships freight by air? And you won't have to do it all yourself, you will find anonymous little helpers who will start planting bombs on planes just for jolly—wouldn't you after reading all about it? They know it's the thing to do, and every device intercepted increases the terror. Then you hit trains and ships, buses and subways inside the cities; you make truck driving the most dangerous profession, with special attention to food trucks; then you can hit the power stations and water reservoirs.

Chemical and biological weapons

For random terror attacks gas bombs are often more effective than explosives; they're also cheaper and easier to make. A container of sulfuric acid concealed in package or briefcase, you press down a plunger which drops sodium cyanide into the acid and leave your package in the subway at the rush hour, or in a theater, or political rally, or revival meeting.

Chemical and biological weapons can be made in the basement lab if you know how.

In *The Wild Boys*, my next novel, I propose to transfer desirable species of plants, animals, fish, and birds from present distribution to other areas where conditions are sufficiently similar to insure growth and reproduction. Look at the map, and always remember your subjects may be more adaptable than you realize. Consider the walleyed pike, which is not a pike but a species of perch and undoubtedly one of the greatest freshwater panfish, found in the lakes and rivers of Minnesota and Canada and in clear cold streams down into Missouri and Arkansas. And consider the small-mouthed black bass of similar distribution. Both species will live in cold water anywhere; they would thrive in the lakes and rivers of England and Scotland and Northern Europe. To the best of my knowledge no one has bothered to import fingerlings. The large-mouthed black bass tolerates quite warm waters and could be extended to the vast waterways of the Amazon basin to the lakes of Africa and South East Asia. The Yage vine could grow in the jungles of South Eastern Asia, in Africa and probably in Louisiana, Florida, and Texas. The delicate lemurs of Madagascar, shy little wood spirits would enhance any rain forest. Certainly the enchanting flying fox deserves wider circulation. Look at the map again—introduction of a new species into an area where it was hitherto unknown can have far reaching consequences. This aspect of biologic warfare has been neglected. Here is the bushmaster from Panama, south through the Amazon basin. He may reach a length of 14 feet and attack a human, twisting about his thighs while he strikes the chest and throat, walking his great fangs that can shoot half a jigger glass of venom. No amount of anti-venom can save him, there isn't time for it to act. Florida, East Texas, Louisiana, Florida, jungles of Africa, South East Asia, the East Indies, and back along the same trade routes—the black mamba of Africa. It will also attack unprovoked, sliding down from trees. Leopards and tigers, released in South America, would soon be driven to maneating by the scarcity of game, and they would eat the CIA men first, since they are bigger and slower. The good grey lard they call it, licking the blood off each others' faces—plentiful, helpless, no fur, the ideal food animal. The fresh water shark of Nicaragua and the piranha[10] fish would do well in the lakes and rivers of Africa, in the Southern United States and South East Asia. For arid regions, the desert cobra, the rattler, and the Gila monster, and the incomparable tiger snake of Australia. And wolverines for Siberia; they are a perfect curse, known to trappers as the "little fiend." And microscopic and submicroscopic life of course, which brings us to biologic warfare proper. The deadly Naga virus[11] is up for grabs, nobody knows how it is transmitted and that gives the virus an advantage which any virus well knows how to take. You immunize your own boys and turn the virus loose, then another, another, until you make the world safe for men of your caliber. No—you don't have to dream up anything from science fiction, the old standbys will go a long way: cholera, typhoid, hepatitis. (It was General Hepatitis who stopped Rommel[12] in North Africa in World War II. There were cartoons depicting General Mud and General Mountains—General Mud if I remember correctly was supposed to stop[13] Hitler in Poland, but his performance was not impressive.) Consignments of ticks carrying Rocky Mountain spotted fever, typhus lice, and of course you go on looking for the big one, a strain of smallpox that thrives on vaccination. Or, suppose you could speed up the time of the process, instead of symptoms spread over a week they are compressed into hours, people swell up with cancer and rot with galloping leprosy on commuter trains.

And now introducing two promising newcomers that deserve your attention—easily and cheaply assembled, from readily available materials. For infrasound and DOR, opportunity knocks. Infrasound: this weapon is fully described in *The Job* published by Jonathan Cape, scheduled for April by Grove Press of New York.[14] So much for the commercial. Infrasound is sound at frequency below the level of human hearing which sets up vibrations in any solid obstruction including the human body. Professor Gavreau,[15] the discoverer of this novel weapon, says that his installation, which resembles a police whistle 18 feet long, can kill up to five miles in any direction, knock down walls and break windows and set off burglar alarms for miles around. His device is patented and anybody can obtain a copy of the plans on payment of 200 francs at the patent office. So, why be a small time sniper? DOR—Deadly Orgone Radiation—produced when any fissionable material is placed in an orgone accumulator. An orgone accumulator is constructed by lining any organic[16] container with sheet iron or steel wool. The container must be of organic material and for full concentration many alternate layers can be used. For full description see the collective works of Dr. Wilhelm Reich.[17] In the chapter entitled "Orgone Physics," Reich says: "There is no protection whatsoever against DOR, since it penetrates everything, including lead or brick or stone walls of any thickness. A criminal hater of mankind or a political enemy, if he knew about this, and if the USA did *not* know about it or did *not* study these effects, could easily drop activated DOR devices looking simply like metal-lined boxes. These could infest a whole region, if not a whole continent. Each person falling ill would react to his or her specific disease or disposition to disease, driving the symptoms to high acuity and then curing them if properly and conscientiously applied. However, if used with malignant intent such infestation of the atmosphere would surely kill or at least immobilize many people." Exposure on a gradient scale gives immunity. Be prepared.

Weapons of disruption, agitation, and subversion

A French Revolutionary sets forth a method by which one man with an unlimited expense account can bring down a goverment. He invents an underground, planting stickers and slogans; acts of sabotage at widely separated locations give an impression that the underground is widespread and well organized. All distubances, strikes, accidents are claimed by the mythical underground. This method might work in an old-style dictatorship like Spain, Greece, Santo Domingo, Haiti. For the complex set up in America and Western Europe you need a whole script and eventually a whole film set.

Notes on writing World Revolution written March 25, 1970, Paris, France.

General Plan

1. An independence, republican, or reform party of exemplary behavior and moderation, staying always within the law. Personnel must be at all times above reproach, at least in the initial stages of the operation. 2. A terrorist underground complete with detailed personnel and methods of operation. Posed films of underground drilling can be leaked to press. The police can be allowed to capture extensive files, taken from a telephone book, and while they drag bewildered citizens from their beds the underground, which consists of a small group of expert saboteurs, can strike somewhere else. 3. A terrorist Right complete with personnel—any outrage can be attributed to these characters. You can see how this works out in present-time Brazil, where any murder of underworld figures can be laid to the terrorist police organization.

The script is different for every country or area of operation. But it is always a 1. 2. 3.

Here is the schema for the United Kingdom.

[1.]¹⁸ An English Republican party, ERP Offices in Bedford Square. Visible personnel must be above reproach. The appeal is rational, stressing economic factors. The monarchy is simply out of keeping with the realities of modern life. Time to forget a dead empire and build a living republic. Stabilize economy, cut expenses, especially defense, let the Yanks and NATO carry that ball, it's too heavy for us. Build up tourist trade by giving them someplace to stay and room service round the clock and food fit to eat. Let's start bringing England into the 20th century. Attract foreign capital, stabilize population by setting up liaison committees to facilitate immigration from the UK to South America—the only underpopulated country. Smooth patter, discreet lunches at Rules and Simpson's.¹⁹ ERP scrupulously abstains from any personal attacks on the Royal Family.

2. We prepare a pamphlet with obscene cartoons covering the Royal Family with vile abuse. We send it out to members of all the best clubs, Conservative MPs, Officers and Gentlemen on Her Majesty's Service. The first wave takes a heavy toll in heart attacks and apoplexy in the halls of drafty clubs, muttering imprecations at yellowing tusks on the wall, walking down country lanes swinging umbrellas and sticks at the air. England is in ferment like a vast vat of bitters. 3. This vile attack on Her Majesty.

Put an end to permissiveness.
Bring back hanging.
Bring back flogging.

The piper plays "Bring Back My Bonnie to Me" on a tin flute down King's Road. 1. ERP deplores pamphlets as sophomoric and calls on the invisible author to desist, which he does of course—the right hand sees what the left hand is doing. A lull during which ERP consolidates gains. ERP, ERP, ERP. Cool, expert patter belching it out all over England. After all, why all this fuss about something left over from the Middle Ages? Just a question of getting people used to it, like the new ten shilling piece. I mean, when we can cut rates and give decent housing they'll forget all about it—the new generation never heard of such a thing. Turn Buckingham Palace into a luxury hotel—one of a chain, and that's where your firm comes in. The Royal Family to be absorbed into the diplomatic service, which is also due for cutbacks and drastic overhaul. Old-style diplomacy dates back to the 18th century and we want to see less goodwill tours and handshaking and more understanding on basic exchange of goods and services. Yes, the whole structure needs overhauling. Why not bring England into the 20th century? Scrap the licensing laws—food and service round the clock. Good middlepriced restaurants like Horn and Hardart.[20] ERP, ERP, ERP! Skinheads, street-gangs, we'll give them something better to do than Paki-bashing and fighting each other—there is useful work for these boys to do.

2. Infiltrate street gangs as first move towards taking over the streets. We send our boys trained in every technique of hand-to-hand fighting and use of weapons and demolition procedures. Jimmy the doctor with a scalpel up his sleeve, electric Kris[21] ready in his boot. These boys assume leadership of street gangs.

"Why fight each other—why not fight the bastards who keep you here in your cold, gritty dank slums? I say bugger the Queen, and anybody doesn't like it just step forward and say so."

These boys have a double mission. First, to put street fighters in the street when we give the word. Riots, burning cars, broken windows, that is the work of the rank and file. Second, they will sift street gangs for the smartest, sharpest, hardest boys to forge the SS,[22] the Palace Guard of ERP. The boys will be exhaustively trained in all fighting techniques and psychological warfare and crowd control. At the right time they will be provided with uniforms, motor cycles, armored cars, and automatic weapons. There is useful work for these boys to do.

Start assassination by list. We drop quite a few red herrings, of course—always leave the door open to blame it all on Rightist plotters. Besides, enigmatic assassinations are more upsetting somehow. We have a tentative list of the real higher-ups in England. As we start working through it, other higher-ups will betray themselves to the trained observer, so the list keeps growing. We will need that list when the time rolls around for *mass* murder, *mass* assassination, MA, and we turn our boys loose.

[3.][23] Now we need a scenario for the Rightist plot. Officers and gentlemen they call themselves, OG. Using American techniques of thought control, they will make the queen a goddess. Her power is absolute. Every citizen must display at all times in his lapel, hat band, shirt or other garment, where it can be plainly seen, the Queen's Rating. QR determines position in her society, imposed at all times. Her favorites all have top rating. They can walk into any restaurant and the manager has to provide a table. They can walk into any hotel and ask for a suite and the manager just has to move somebody out.

Intolerable little cockney faggot in 18th-century costume with a powdered blue wig and a snuff-box full of cocaine: "Get this low-rate riff-raff out of my suite."

And so it goes on down the scale to the dreaded pariah rating, PR, which is tattooed in red ink on the forehead like the brand of Cain. Anyone can refuse to serve food, grant lodging, or take in any public transport a PR. And so her loyal and loyaler subjects think twice about incurring²⁴ her serene displeasure. And it is well to remember that her favor is not to be taken for granted but must be earned anew each day.

Actually the queen is simply a holograph symbol of subservience manipulated by American knowhow. Vulgar chaps by and large, but they do have the technology. Recent experiments with rhesus monkeys have demonstrated that fear, rage, excretory processes and sexual response can be brought under pushbutton control. The Chinese delegate screams with rage and shits in his pants on TV. The Soviet delegate masturbates uncontrollably. Early answer to use on anyone considering to interfere. We set it all up with top-secret documents, statements from a former CIA man who must for his own safety remain anonymous, and we put our rumor boys into the street with tape recorders.

1. England is taking orders from the CIA and the American Narcotics Department like a Central American banana republic. Wouldn't surprise me to see the marines land. Look at this drug problem they've dumped in our lap. Go after the pushers, you arrest one pusher and ten more will take his place. The one man the narcotics industry can't do without is the addict in the street who buys it. Treat the addict in the street and you'll put the pusher out of busi-

ness. The apomorphine treatment started in England. Why not give it a chance in England and let's give these kids something better to do. Why not reverse the brain drain? It isn't just more money that takes our best research brains to America, it's better equipment and opportunities for more advanced research. The new work in autonomic shaping carried out in America by doctors Engel, Kamiya, Neill, and Laing—they are teaching subjects to control brain waves, rate of heart beat, blood pressure, digestive processes and sexual response. This could lead to trips without drugs and solve the drug problem. Is England picking up? Is similar research being carried out at Bristol Neurological Foundation by Professor Gray Walters?[25] If so, we haven't heard about it. Is England afraid of any research that could turn up something basically new? Is England muddling through or simply muddling steadily downhill? Is the mismanagement we see here part of a deliberate plot? It's beginning to look that way.

2. Riots and demonstrations by street gangs are stepped-up. Start random assassinations. Five citizens every day in London, but never a police officer or a serviceman. Patrols in the street, shooting the wrong people. Curfews. England is rapidly drifting towards anarchy.

3. We send out our best agents to contact Army Officers and organize a Rightist coup. We put Rightist gangs into it like the Royal Crowns and the Royal Cavaliers[26] in the streets.

1. Time for ERP to come out in the open. The trouble with England is, it is run by old women of both sexes. We have a list of these people, we will not allow them to use the army to overthrow constitutional government and impose a dictatorship under pretense of controlling the disorders which they themselves have caused. It is time for young England to strike, and strike hard. We turn our palace guard loose.

An armored car draws up in front of Claridges.[27] Youths with tommy guns jump out and block off the street. A TV crew unloads. The whole scene goes out live on TV. Steps through the silent dining room stop by a table. A burst of machine-gun fire, a woman screams. "Shut up, you whore. And now will you all please stand up. That's right. Now all of you sing 'God Save The Queen.'" Boys walk around the dining room. "You there! Louder! More soul!" The car stops in front of the best club of them all. (It's not White's I'm told but we'll be around to White's[28] later.) They'll be waiting, the old gentlemen in their armchairs muttering about permissiveness, in the writing room writing letters to urge the restoration of hanging and flogging. The boys leap out in their natty blue uniforms with a skull and cross bones at the lapel that glows in the dark.

"Are you a member, sir?"

The boy shoots him coldly in the stomach with a P38. It's nice for city wear, so much more elegant than a revolver. Quick, purposeful young steps down drafty halls, tusks all over the wall, the improbable hyphenated names. The members are frozen. What *is* this outrage, when a gentleman is reading his *Times*? They expect the club steward to come and throw the bounders out, perhaps it's even a case for the bobbies. The steps stop in front of an armchair.

"Are you Lord Stansfield?"[29]

"I am."

He's the most intelligent person in the room—intelligent enough to know that this is serious. The boy is very elegant and disengaged. Lord Stansfield decides to try a paternal approach.

"Son."

The boy gives him a short burst across the chest. The diving bell of the 19th century, shattered by a boy's bullets. The members are numb from the shock wave. TV camera, floodlights. The boy paces around the vast lounge looking at the pictures. He points the gun at a steward's stomach.

"You there, bring champagne."

"Champagne, sir?"

"Yes, champagne, and glasses for all the officers and gentlemen, the servants as well, and don't be forgetting the military."

The trembling steward passes around the clicking glasses.

"You there, pick it up."

Now the boy stands in front of the Queen's picture. He raises his glass.

"Bugger the Queen."

He throws the empty glass at the picture, shards of glass sticking into the Queen's face. The members are frozen. The boy unslings his tommy gun and shoots down five members in a random sequence, pivoting from the hip. He picks up another glass.

"And now all you officers and gentlemen, gather round here. That's right I want to hear it, I want to hear it good and loud. Bugger the Queen!"

All over England, the elite guard carry the message of death. They have some natty uniforms with trick gadgets. A skull and cross bones in the lapel and helmet that winks on and off, and blue revolving skull lights on the cars. And some frantic faggots get themselves up in skeleton suits, of course, sweeping down country roads. Thirty boys on motor cycles draw up in front of a stately home.

"Yes, sir?"

"Where is the old bitch?"

The butler's face does not change.

"Mrs. Charington[30] is in the garden, sir."

And there she is in her trowels and slacks, digging away at her roses.

"What do you want, young man?"

She thinks he will quail before a good woman's gaze. He doesn't.

"Lebensraum,[31] you old hag, you poison the air we breathe."

Mrs. Charington bleeds into her roses. The butler is busy with a wall safe.

They sweep up to a baronial Scottish estate.

"You'll have to wait constable, the family is at dinner."

"Good, so we'll join them."

Jabs the butler in the stomach with his tommy gun. The lord and lady die in their seats, faces in the grouse. The Children, a boy of 18 and a girl of 16, sit there,[32] faces blank with shock.

Slowly the boy's face glows and sharpens with calculation, his lips part, and his eyes shine. Two truths are told as happy preludes to the swelling act. And now for my unfortunate brother.

Lead boy calls in two footmen.

"Bring mattresses. You and you, go along and see they don't get lost."

Television cameras set up, the mattresses brought in and dropped on the floor in front of the fireplace.

Next scene shows the other boys gang-fucking the girl while the new boy tries on his new uniform.

All over England, under the searching guns pubs echo to

"BUGGER THE QUEEN"

Taken up by junkies, meth heads, hippies, played back on recorders, live on TV,

"BUGGER THE QUEEN"

Rises to the pale English sky. Whole regiments scream it out.

"BUGGER THE QUEEN"

And murder their officers straight away.

Boy packs with tommy guns march down the street and blast every shop window that bears the hated placard "By appointment to Her Majesty the Queen." And everyone they meet had better scream it out loud.

"BUGGER THE QUEEN"

They march into offices, schools, factories, apartment houses,

"Alright all of you, stick your head out the window and show some respect,"

"BUGGER THE QUEEN"
All over England, heads pop out of windows, screaming
"BUGGER THE QUEEN"
Languid young officers on flower floats parade through
the streets as the delirious populace chants
"BUGGER THE QUEEN"
Bugger the Queen is now the national greeting.
ERP occupies Buckingham Palace to protect and advise
the Royal Family. Decimated by assassination and deprived
of psychic support, the army falters. The Queen abdi-
cates while the elite guard languidly polish their nails on
skull lapels. And who is that in a *very natty* tailor-made
uniform?[33]

No, it was not a difficult decision to issue these licenses
for rape and murder. Nothing more ominous than a difficult
decision in the Pentagon. And nobody does more harm than
he who feels bad about doing it. Sad poison nice guy, more
poison than nice, wept when he saw the Hiroshima pictures.
What a drag, when we murder someone we want to have
fun doing it.

This license was dictated by a consideration taken into
account by prudent commanders throughout history. You
have to pay the boys off. Even the noble Brutus did it.

"The town is yours boys."

Tacitus[34] describes a typical scene. "If a young girl or
good-looking boy fell into their hands they were torn to
pieces in the struggle for possession, and the survivors were
left to cut each other's throats." Well, there is no need for it
to be that messy. Why waste a good-looking boy? Mother-
loving American Army run by old women, many of them
religious, *my god.* Hanging American soldiers for raping and
murdering civilians.

"WHAT THE BLOODY FUCKING HELL ARE CIVIL-
IANS FOR?"

Old Sarge bellows from here to eternity:

"SOLDIERS' PAY."

The CO stands there and smiles. Just ahead is a middle-western American town, about 200,000. A pretty town, on a river, plenty of trees. The CO points.

"It's all yours boys, every man, woman and child of it. Anything in it, living or dead."

"Now just a minute boys, listen to old Sarge. Why make the usual stupid scene kicking in liquor stores, grabbing anything in sight? You wake up with a hangover in an alley, your prick tore from fucking dry cunts and assholes, your eye gouged out by a broken beer bottle, you and your buddie wanted the same one. No fun in that. Why not leave it like it is? They go about their daily tasks and we just take what we want when we want it, cool and easy and make them like it, you see what I mean? 5,000 of us, 200,000 of them."

A young lieutenant in camouflage sees what he means. Boys, school showers and swimming pools full of them.

"So we lay it on the line. There's no cause for alarm folks, proceed about your daily tasks. But one thing is clearly understood your lives, your bodies, your properties belong to us whenever and wherever we choose to take them. So we weed out the undesirables and turn the place into a paradise. Getting it steady year after year. Now that's what I call pay."

Ideally, mass assassination, MA, should be worldwide.[35]

SLAUGHTER THE SHITS OF THE WORLD, THEY POISON THE AIR WE BREATHE.

You know who they are in America, 20 years minimum for possession of marihuana, decent church-going nigger-killing crackers, and don't forget the womenfolk is worse than the men. Decency leagues, anti-obscenity drives, they poison the air we breathe. You know who they are. John Birch[36] billionaires, newspaper owners, finking[37] cab drivers and hotel clerks, narks and ghetto landlords, acid-throwing Mafia wops,[38] any bastard connected with MRA,[39] all the servants and guard dogs and company cops of the rich.

We intend a total solution to the shit problem. They claim their shit world is the way things are and force it on the rest of us with police terror. Slaughter these shits and the face of the world will smile. And what will we do with all the dead shits? Grind them up and process them into high protein hog feed, and grind their bones into bonemeal for our fields and lawns and gardens. They comprise between 10 and 20 percent of the world population, though in heavily infected areas like South Africa it may run much higher. About the only good Boer[40] is a processed one, feeding our happy hogs. Start slaughtering the shits of the world and you will see how much better everybody feels right away, some looks are simply good right there. It's a shitty world they tell us, always was and always will be, part of a great plan. We don't like this plan. Slaughter the shits and feel the difference. Slaughter the shits in all walks of life. Now it may be an evil old bitch spitting venom from her tobacco kiosk, London, Paris, Madrid. It may be a cab driver won't take pop stars in from the airport, he doesn't want that lot in his cab. And we don't want you on our lot cabbie, because you are a shit. It may be a billionaire who contributes to MRA and keeps a stable of stringy, constipated, spam-eating Christers in South America infecting healthy Indians. It's just like killing a cow with the Aftosa[41] slobbering it all over everybody else. It may be a doorman of a good club. "Are you a member, sir?" Club his shitty brains out. It may be a ghetto landlord, they are hard to find but our black brothers will find them. Or it may be a southern lawman chuckling over his nigger-notches. Religious women, decency leagues, anti-obscenity drives, you poison the air we breathe. Wipe out the bible belt and you will glimpse the Garden of Eden.

"It was like being cured of clap after twenty dripping years," said a dazed bystander. Happy smiling faces from sea to shining sea.[42]

And now, back to merry England and getting merrier by the minute, as the shit slaughter guard goes to work.

Office of the SS Demolition Unit.

Investigation has convinced us that the so-called Neurological and Encephalographic Institute is emitting shit brainwaves on a massive basis.

Old duffer there hasn't turned up anything useful in twenty years. No work with autonomic shaping. We urge an immediate therapeutic test. Cut off his power.

To a rousing rendition of altered reality, old men dance naked in the streets.

"YIPPEE THIS IS THE FIRST HARD ON I'VE HAD IN TWENTY YEARS."

Others show symptoms of asphyxia as if an invisible air line had been cut, and many die from the abrupt withdrawal of shit.

A car draws up in front of University College, London. The SS Demolition Unit gets out. Jeremy Bentham,[43] mummified head of.

"Right through there, sir, at the end of the hall, sir. You can't miss it, sir, it stinks something awful, sir. Especially in summer, sir."

The guard advances to a position three feet in front of the head. He levels a 12 gauge sawed-off shotgun and cuts loose with two barrels of heavy duckload.[44]

"And take those dirty old mummies out of the British Museum and dump them down a marl hole."[45]

Mass orgies and other wholesome manifestations break out all over London.

In all walks of life[46] the SS Personnel Units do their work. In the stately homes and the best clubs, in kiosks, shops, pubs, and coffee bars. A witch hunt? Exactly. Four or five evil old biddies can bring down a whole quarter of London. The SS does its work and goes. They leave behind them happy smiling faces and hearts at peace under an English heaven. Memory of what has been and never more will be. Soon even the memory of those shits will fade into air. Into thin air. The fields of England are heavy and rich with their bone meal, and our happy hogs are fat and firm with their flesh.

Now to put our program in operation.

The food in England is now fit only for the consumption of an underprivileged vulture. We will give people good food. Of course, our world famous shit-fed hogs are a long step in that direction. Long pig, we call it. And if there's one thing England has, it's plenty of water, so build fish ponds everywhere and stock them with bass and jack salmon and perch. England becomes an anglers' paradise. Close down some factories too, we won't need them with the tourist business we'll soon be doing.

We will give people a place to live. Weeding out 5 million shits is a long step in that direction. All out birth control, level off the population at 20 million.

We will give people good sex. The first step is to bring people with reciprocal tastes, objectives together. We set up community centers for the exchange of home sex movies and tapes. We set up computerized guidance centers. At the Sexual Institute we teach people how to enjoy sex. Brain waves, heart rate, blood pressure, electrical impulses from the penis are precisely charted. We now know exactly what the subject wants and now we find someone with precisely reciprocal reactions. We teach people to emit sex brain waves at will. These are probably the alpha-rhythms which occur during sleep. We stage sex festivals where 400,000 naked people gather together and emit sex brain waves. Real sex on stage and screen. As Mr. Hubbard[47] says, the way out is the way through. Our experiments at the Sexual Institute will soon show us what sex is all about, then we can go beyond it.

And now for the real job. What are we here for?

Brion Gysin answers this question in *The Process*,[48] recently published by Jonathan Cape in England and Doubleday in America. We are here to go! The real job is space. Let's chart inner space and explore outer space. The first step towards exploring inner space is to learn control of your own mind and body.

The discipline of DE[49] is taught in all schools, together with Alexander's system of proper use of the head-neck relationship. Control of mind and body can be carried further by autonomic shaping. American scientists have taught subjects to control blood pressure, rate of heart beat, brain waves, digestion, and sexual response. Any trip you like is now possible without drugs. Unimaginable extensions of awareness are now possible in terms of existing techniques. Let's set up centers where these techniques are pooled and interchanged. Can man leave his body without incurring physical death?

"No!" the shits scream, "If he could do that we couldn't keep him working in our offices and factories."

We call in all the wizards and warlocks, and shamans and witchdoctors and mediums and table tappers. The English eccentric flourishes as never before in history. The hallucinogenic drugs described in *The Teachings of Don Juan* by Carlos Castaneda,[50] out here in Penguin paperback, are isolated and the corresponding brain waves charted. This is a fun program. This is the adventure of space. Who is standing in the way of such a program? The shits of the world. Slaughter the shits of the world, then we can all have some fun for a change.

MA is of course a utopian fantasy. To return to the realities of the present time. Centers can be set up by pooling private funds, just as balloon and glider clubs pool resources to make balloons and gliders available to the contributing members. It is not surprising that balloon and glider clubs united by a common purpose have been more successful than centers set up for more general cultural purposes. The centers proposed, the research to be carried out, equipment necessary, is described in detail in *The Job* and in the present treatise.

Aim of training is to decondition subject from past conditioning, which is automatic, and to bring all his abilities under his control—including so-called automatic processes such as rate of heart beat, blood pressure, brain waves, and sexual responses. The projects will cover tape recorders and video cameras, speech scramblers, autonomic shaping, various forms of physical training. A linguistic institute to create a new language and an institute to create a new calendar.

Centers have failed in the past because their objectives were too vague. Our objectives are quite definite. A program of research and a system of training to produce an improved human product. So much improved that no old training method can compete.

There are other reasons than vagueness as to overall or even short-term objectives for the frequent failure of such centers, seemingly inexplicable since they obviously could fill a need felt by many people. One reason is undoubtedly infiltration by official agents allegedly checking on drug abuse or subversive political activities, actually there to sabotage the centers. Remember that such centers are subversive by nature so far as the control machine is concerned. Such sabotage is very easy. Set key figures against each other and so forth. Remember they have nothing else to do. Another reason for failure is simply lack of competence of the people involved. If they cannot function on a professional level, professionals are put off; nothing interesting seems to be going on and the descending spiral sets in as fewer and fewer serious workers find the center worthwhile. How can these difficulties be overcome?

1.⁵¹ The actual objectives of any center, any part or project under a center, should be as clearcut and definite as possible. The elimination of infiltrators can be accomplished by an E meter test. This instrument costs about £50 and can be purchased at any scientology center. In expert hands it is an infallible lie detector and no one proposing to use the center should object to its use. Are you here for any other reason than what you say you are? Are you connected to any official agencies? These questions must be checked on the E meter. One infiltrator can wreck a project, and projects proposed to put the establishment out of business can expect infiltrators. Don't let one in. A professional level of competence must be insisted upon by those taking part in research programs and handling equipment. Otherwise the project will founder and you will not see results.[52]

Now it isn't every country has a sitting duck like the Royal Family. Bugger the President doesn't make it at all. The script is quite different for the United States of America. No. 1. The job party. JP. Vote, don't riot.

We call it the JP because if there's one thing America stands for it is doing the job, and they just aren't doing the job. Take a look at the so-called drug problem, and think in terms of doing the job. Suppose you are running a business. The traffic department is a mess and can't get shipments in and out. "We need more personnel," they say. So you give them more personnel and the snarl gets worse, and more and more personnel and the snarl gets worse, and worse, and worse. How long would I go on doing that? Twice maybe. Then I fire the whole traffic department from top to bottom. I call in Genua[53] drummers to drive out the evil spirits and change the filing system. I promise all of you that JP will fire every nark in America. The grey dikes have nothing to recommend them but their bad statistics. This no-knock drug bill gives them the right to break in any door with a sledge hammer, day or night. Nor need they necessarily come in at the door. They can drive a bulldozer through your wall or pop up through the floor. And the bill gives them control over all narcotics research programs. What has the research program of Lexington[54] turned up over thirty years of spending the taxpayers' money? Not even methadon. They got that from the Germans in World War II. Have they come up with any workable treatment? They have not. Fire the whole research department and put someone in there who does the job. Let's get together with communist China, and stop giving the taxpayers' money to bastards like Chiang Kaichek.[55] Let's stop all atomic testing. Cut the defense budget. Concentrate on space. That's what young people want. They want adventure, something important to do. We are going to give it to them.

As you see, the approach here is quite different. Number 1 is much more openly allied with number 2 than was deemed prudent in the initial stages of the English operation.

No. 2. There are many militant and terrorist groups already in operation. We postulate that these units are all acting under a unified plan and by postulating and writing the plan we bring it into operation. Start assassination by list. In no country is ABL more important since the real higher-ups have got themselves hit[56] good, and for very good reasons.

No. 3. There are many Rightist Terrorist groups already in operation. Once again, we unify these groups by attributing them to one malignant intelligence: Introducing The Unspeakable Mr. Hart.[57] Before initiating surface operations in any area, it is well to spend at least a year in advance preparations. Stockpiling arms and ammunition, explosives, cyanide and a wide variety of poisons, fissionable materials for DOR[58] installations, phosgene, nerve gas, laser guns and infrasound devices. These operations will become increasingly difficult once JP surfaces and gains ground as a radical party, and JP is much more openly allied with the left than ERP. It is, in fact, quite openly allied with the student left while deploring, at all times, the use of violence. And in this preparatory period the investigative work is carried out to compile the list of targets for individual assassinations. We have dossiers on every name on this list—who they meet, where they go—and we plant an assassin in the office, a new secretary perhaps, in the garden, behind the bar, or in the kitchen, who will strike when the time comes. This is the method devised by Hasan-i Sabbah, the Old Man of the Mountain. A general was about to lead an expedition against Alamut,[59] when he was killed with a scythe by an old man who had worked in his garden for ten years. And we infiltrate the enemy at all levels—police, army, navy, business, mass media, CIA. These undercover agents stand ready for operations of sabotage and murder. They also serve as an intelligence network. Most of them are anonymous, unnoticed, but some may rise to the top in their simulated trade or profession.

And now back to 1. 2. 3. America. In America success depends on the ability of number 1 to obtain the united and active support of the entire liberal left.

"Now politicians are always spouting about what they are going to do if elected, but we are going to start doing it right now."

Number 1 puts out a daily paper and sets up a TV station. We set up reconditioning and community centers. We show how control devices like speech scramblers operate.

No. 2. The role of number 2 is to guard the centers. Of course, the police will take every pretext to raid and close the centers. Here is a raiding party of 20 cops, they are met by 20 karate trained guards.

"We have a search warrent for these premises."

"Alright, we'll show you around."

And everywhere they go video cameras and tape recorders follow their every movement. It won't be easy for them to plant anything.

No. 3. One plot after the other is attributed to number 3, and publicized by number 1. A plot to use DOR, a plot to obtain mass control by using the Reactive Mind and speech scramblers. A plot to drop an old-style atom bomb on New York and San Francisco. That would eliminate a lot of the troublemakers right there. Then we claim a sneak attack by the Chinese, throw all surviving dissenters into concentration camps and the army takes over. Plot to do the same using a nerve gas.[60]

No. 1. There is already a gap between the mass media and the administration in America. We do everything possible to increase this gap towards a takeover of the mass media. There are many possibilities here. We issue a story that the American politicans and their constituents, many of them, have been taken over by a Venusian virus and call upon them to surrender themselves for reconditioning like cows with the Aftosa. We have actors to impersonate the President and the Vice-President as they come in and surrender. The admirals, generals, and industrial giants of America rumble in like sick dinosaurs, the entire bible belt is in quarantine. There are indeed many possibilities here and a takeover without violence in the accepted sense is possible in America, perhaps more possible than in any other area.[61]

There are perhaps forty million people in the United States in such basic disagreement with the present, past, and foreseeable future administrations in this country that they would welcome any positive change. Number 1 must unite the entire liberal left. We issue membership cards and lapel badges. Number 1 must unite the entire liberal left as a voting block. Any candidate for office from alderman to president is carefully screened and the most liberal candidate given the green light.

You have numbers. Use them, the vote is a weapon. Drop in to register and vote. Forty million people could also make the boycott a total weapon. Now, for example, I am disgusted by the *Daily News* editorial pages. The ugly American, crude and rampant, on and on about Mao[62] and his gang of cut-throats—one vulgar, stupid American bray. I am equally disgusted by the editorial page of the *Daily Telegraph,* which is saying exactly the same thing in a quieter English voice. Well, I won't put the *News* out of business by not buying their paper, so I go on buying it for the pictures and the comics. But forty million united people *could* put the *News* out of business. The boycott is announced in the underground press, total boycott on the *Daily News.* TB on the *Daily News.* This means that forty million people stop buying it. This means that any news-stand owner who is one of our own won't stock it. We picket the news-stands that sell it, annoy and insult the customers. Staying within the law, of course. A citizen has a right to say what he wants to say in the public street. TB extends to all personnel and all advertisers. Waiters and bar tenders refuse to serve them, cab drivers won't let them in their cabs, porters won't touch their luggage. TB is just *that*. A total boycott on any company or person connected with, working for, or profiting from the target. It is also a magical operation directing the dislike of forty million people on the target. Any little thing any one of you can do to harass, harm, insult, hold up to ridicule the target will be appreciated. The campaign is carried out with the maximum surface publicity. You dig out their most outrageous editorials and reprint etc. day after day. TB on the *Daily News*. Yes, a boycott like that soon becomes news, and big news and bigger and bigger. Put out a derogatory mutter line on target. Precise instructions for doing this are given in this treatise. Quite a weapon. The target can be a country or it can be an individual. TB on the Greek junta.[63] Don't go to Greece. And we can make it quite uncomfortable for those who do go and for Greek airlines and travel agencies. TB. Directed against an individual, TB can be devastating. A billionaire had to be rescued by heliocopter from his West Indian estate where he was dying of starvation, because nobody would sell him food. And of course, we use TB on rival candidates for office. Yes, as time goes on more and more people are going to want those little badges we give out. Folks will think twice about tangling with a JP badge.

Now for 1, 2, 3, South America.

Here there's no possibility of success without force in its most overt form, namely men with guns. Rulers are all the way out in the open, have been for centuries, and are prepared to maintain their position by force. Number 1 will get nowhere without a well trained and well-armed number 2.

No. 1. The curse of South America is grafting politicans, unnecessary armies, a small ruling class, backed by the Catholic church, who keep the people in poverty and ignorance in what is potentially the richest country in the world. And it is also the only underpopulated country in existence. There is absolutely no valid reason for these separate countries except to maintain armies that impoverish and oppress the people. The whole of South America must be united into one country. South American republics, with the exception of Brazil, share a common language, they also share the same economic problems and, by and large, the same racial stock. South America stands now where America stood a hundred years ago. They can avoid the errors of too rapid[64] indus- trialization such as erosion, air and water pollution, soil exhaustion, concentration of unwieldly population blocks in urban centers, and the whole curse of over-population.

No. 2. The success of number 1 is absolutely dependent on effective guerilla[65] forces. As some of you know there are now more CIA men than guerillas in South America. They infiltrate the guerilla units, machine gun them, or turn them in to the local army units. To guard against this infiltration we institute security checks with an E meter. In expert hands the E meter is an infallible lie detector. Here is a jungle camp, the CIA infiltrator is conducted to a hut, around the walls are the shrunk-down heads of his predecessors. The exam- iner sits at a table with an E meter in front of him, flanked by two guards with tommy guns.

Examiner: "Will you pick up the cans, please. Are you here for any reason other than what you say you are?" That reads, what do you consider this could mean?

CIA man: "Well, it's just that I feel I'm not trusted here."

Examiner: "I'll ask the question again. Are you here for any other reason than what you say you are?" There's another read here, what do you consider this could mean?

CIA man: "Well, uh, I guess we all have different ideas as to what we want from the revolution."

Examiner: "Are you connected with the CIA?" That rock slams, what do you consider this could mean?

CIA man: "It's just that the whole idea is ridiculous."

Examiner: "Is this a protest read? Is this a protest read? No it is not a protest read, I will ask the question again. Are you connected with the CIA?" That reads, what do you con- sider this could mean?

A hand places the CIA man's shrunk-down head on a shelf.

An efficient intelligence system is also essential to the operation of number 2. In many cases, a known CIA agent can be more useful alive than dead to pass on false information, and lead government troops into ambushes. Intelligence agents can also infiltrate the army and the police. No. 3. Many such organizations are already in operation, particularly in Brazil. Continual accusations that the generals and politicians are selling the country out, to the CIA.

Number 1 must find a base of operations that will give them newspaper, radio, and TV facilities. This is done through a Leftist coup by number 2 in a small country like Ecuador. We will call it Republic 2. Refugee generals and politicians from Republic 2 inundate the cocktail lounges of Miami and Washington.

"Yes, we are fighting the tyranny of communism. Yes, I will have another triple whisky."

The taxpayers' money pours into their laps. The newborn Socialist state screams to China and Russia for arms. Next door is Republic 3, a Rightist country, our prop of course. There are border clashes. Number 3 screams to America for arms; weapons and military advisers pour in. Republic 2 and Republic 3 now have the only two modern, well-equipped armies in South America. They join forces, and take over the whole country. They immediately put in practice the reforms suggested by number 1. The liberated area is now united as the land of Mu.[66]

The scenic beauty and variety of scenery offered by this vast continent are I think unparalleled anywhere else on this planet. In the wide Equatorial belt the scenery and climate vary with altitude and can change completely in a few miles of travel. Here is the coastal area of Ecuador—hardwood forest, low hills, wide muddy rivers, country very much like the Ozark Mountains in the southern United States. The rivers here are very much in use and during the rainy season when roads flood out are the only means of travel. Ecuador is unique in this coastal area of hardwood forest that might have been transported from the southern United

States. Squirrel, racoon, possum, wild turkey would flourish in these forests. Large-mouthed black bass and channel cat would thrive in the rivers. As we travel upward the hills are higher, oranges, papaya, and avocado grow wild in profusion. The water is colder here, ideal for perch, smallmouthed bass, and jack salmon. And so up through the bare windswept mountains and down again into the plateau area where most of the Ecuadorian cities are concentrated. Now we start down into the Amazon area. High jungle, cool in the shade, great trees some 200 feet tall, chasms and waterfalls. The Amazon basin comprises the largest reservoir of virgin[67] rain forest. Not much undergrowth here, owing to the shade, clear streams of water everywhere. There are vast plains in the Argentine and Columbia and Venezuela, in the Guianas and Brazil. There are the coastal deserts of Peru where rain is unknown, and the lunar landscape of Chile. In this whole area, largely unindustrialized, unpolluted, and under populated, the possibilities for building beautiful towns and cities are breathtaking. Redbrick cities in the coastal areas of Ecuador. Arab architecture would be admirably suited to the coastal deserts. In the Amazon area houseboat cities and river towns. There is every variety of wood to build houses—oak, mahogany, and the heavy woods that must be worked with metal tools. Old time riverboats stock the Amazon and its vast tributories.[68] Our borders thrown open to architects, writers, artists, scientists and technicians, no nonsense about permits—come and stay as long as you like, or accept a lucrative position doing really important research in all directions.

Oh, we aren't just peace and love and everybody doing his thing.

We are not that short-sighted.

We know that the so-called free world will attack Mu on any pretext. So everybody comes to Mu, taxes are low, pot is legal, jets rain down from the skies and dot our harbors with yachts and the local youths shine with star saphires. And, needless to say, we incur the bitter envy of less colorful tourist centers. Behind this glittering facade, in experimental communes and laboratories the research goes on. The whole land of Mu is a vast experimental project in human variety. Introducing Herr Doktor Kurt von Steinplatz: "In these all-male communes it was our project to create so beings without fear. To be without womans is to be without fear—is it not? These boys have been raised from birth in an all-male environment, from which even the pictures of womans are excluded. We had at first the maternal clinic and much trouble with the womans, they should shut up the mouth and not continually blab, blab every fearsome thing they can think up or remember, so to poison the unborn child with their words. So for nine months you can shut up, hein? But when we attempted to impose a rule of silence in the clinic the womans showed signs of acute asphyxiation, so bringing our sex determined males in peril. We tell them then, alright talk, but we will tell you what to talk, and rig them up to a random program. Now, thank god, we work from cuttings and slides. So the communes are all different in their customs and way of life. We expect actual mutations. The third generation of boys what has never seen a woman is so another animal, perhaps in two or three hundred years. To create so beings without fear is against the will of the creator, hein? He has a great plan for our salvation to grovel for all eternity, is it not? His bible-belt cattle would trample my work. Let the creator come forth with his so great plan for a universe of fear, where only the strongest, most vicious, treacherous, and cruel can survive. The aggressive southern ape. So, vun[69] bastard after the other clubs and lies and doublecrosses his way to the top of this ugly heap. In *The Heart of the Matter*[70] Mr. Greene speaks of the terrible weakness of God. The terrible weakness of a tapeworm that feeds on shit and piss in the pants from fear, humiliations, and kicks in the nuts. The foul[71] flag of Sodom floats brazenly over the so-called land of Mu, wrested from the rightful and lawful governments of South America by Communist cut-throats, perverts, and drug addicts who now boast of raising children from birth in the practice of unnatural vices. The land of Mu flies not only the flag of Sodom naked and unashamed, and I may add, adequately protected. In remote valleys are so communes of exquisite Lesbians known as Dike Ferns, where[72] they live in little tile houses and twitter away like birds, it is vun of our tourist attractions. And there is in the high mountains some groups of womans which has got themselves up like Valkyrie. Ve have also sex centers where all sexes commingle in combos to produce so the bestest comings for the mostest fuckers. You see it is all healthy and good fun, hein? You do not like good fun in the bible-belt?" (Some of the bible-belt men went slackjawed and speculative, but what they was thinkin' died under a good woman's gaze.) "You will find that we are no longer banana republics and when it comes to throw the rotten eggs." He leans across his desk with a fragile yellow egg, there is something black boiling inside it. "Yes, any small country with a good bio-chemist can now make the virus for which there is no cure— the coded message of death contained here in this so fragile egg. I have but to throw it and pup! But we are civilized men and do not like to harm innocent people. American jungens so with freckles, the leg hairs shiny, pimples on the ass. We have so another wunderbar thing, a virus of silence which is attacking the vocal chords and the speech centers in the brain and millions die from the abrupt inability to scream out. Permissiveness, dope fiend, communist, queer—so like a big towel stopping all the big mouths of the world. And here is this a rottenest egg. We have here the right virus."

Scene outside a Southern American town. A young white man staggers out onto a road and falls to his knees. Armed negros watch him.

"Alright, Rightie, keep your distance."

He looks up. "Listen, I'm not one of them, I tell you it hit town last night and suddenly my old lady starts screaming out she is RIGHT, RIGHT, RIGHT. And I say, sure you are honey face, so why don't you let up aggravatin' me and fix dinner. But she just goes on hollerin', bringing it up from her guts the way it made all the windows rattle. So I tied her to a chair and went out to fetch Doc Sherman. He should come in and give her a shot a' something and shut her up. When I get out in the street I see it is happening everywhere. It's like a movie I seen once called "The Night of the Living Dead."[73] "They won't last the night—here come some now."

A group of men and women stagger out on to the road. They move with galvanic disjointed arms and legs, gesticulating, muttering, and screaming out from time to time RIGHT, RIGHT, RIGHT. The words tearing their throats out, they fall spitting blood and die in bone-wrenching spasms.

And here is another.

A routine narcotics raid. Eight narks bash in a door and step in with their guns out—just an act of course, they don't expect to use them.

"Alright—this is a narcotics bust. Stay where you are."

A youth with cold metallic eyes whips a 38 from his waistband and kills three cops before he goes down under a hail of bullets.

Next scene is a laboratory, chemist and special agent on set.

Chemist: "This is not heroin, but it is a variation on the heroin formula. We have just run preliminary animal experiments. Animals injected with this drug died in convulsions if the drug was withheld for more than five hours. The injection of large doses of heroin did not affect the symptoms. This drug is perhaps a hundred times more habit-forming than heroin and also of course a hundred times as effective as a pain killer. As you know, pain no amount of codeine can relieve, is effectively relieved by morphine and pain which morphine cannot relieve is relieved by heroin. Two types of pain are not relieved by any known anelgesics:[74] these are leprosy of the eye and certain fish poisons described as like fire in the blood. Now imagine the degree of pain that could not be relieved by a drug[75] ten times stronger than heroin.

"Capture[76] for such an addict means death in literally inconceivable agony. Even if the police were willing to administer heroin no amount of heroin could save the addict from a horrible death. So they will go to any lengths to avoid capture.[77] Also remember the degree of immunity from pain this drug affords. It must be a condition where pain and fear are suspended. Possibly a condition approaching a mineral consciousness. The heroids may prove very efficient indeed, and they have every reason to infect others for their own protection."

Next scene shows a whistling milkman, loading milk into his truck. Black jack, change of uniforms, the milk truck goes out. In the back a stony-faced youth injects a few drops into every bottle with an air-pressure syringe. Soft drinks stands, bars, resturants, an agent with a racoon coat shakes out heroid dust filling a subway car in the rush-hour. The dust billows from apartment windows and cigarette ads, a crop duster sweeps down Broadway, they're taking over whole areas, setting up factories. In the Pentagon, grim-faced officers consider the emergency. Quarantine lines are falling one after the other. The heroids now occupy a third of America. At the head of the table a 5-star general glares imperiously, two wings perched on his shoulders. Suddenly a jet of heroid gas shoots from each wing.

Next scene shows heroid canisters being loaded into army planes.

We will protect our project. And that project is to produce a variety of humanoid sub-species. This may have happened before. At one time were many humanoid species, and the strongest, meanest, and most bestial only survived. The aggressive southern ape, sir, survived because he was a killer. So we rerun evolution, with a referee this time, who will not take any dumheits[78] from this antiquated ape. New species arise by not knowing, by not knowing the old ways, the old words, the old laws and prohibitions, the so stupid, RIGHT or WRONG.

In the foregoing pages I have described a number of revolutionary weapons, devices, and procedures, clearly recognisable as weapons designed to kill or incapacitate opponents. Revolutionaries, having been forced into armed opposition, are prone to be suspicious of other weapons. If you can't hit someone over the head with it right now they don't want to know. Who are the enemies? The following statement, which was intended to outline the policy of a newspaper to be called MOB, I think will show us who the enemies are.[79]

MY OWN BUSINESS . . . M. O. B. . . . MOB . . . assumes the right of every individual to possess his inner space, to do what interests him with people he wants to see. In some areas this right was more respected a hundred years ago than it is in the permissive society.

"Which is it this time, Holmes? Cocaine or morphine?" asks a disapproving Watson.

But Holmes won't have fink hounds sniffing through his Baker Street digs. If he accepts an American assignment 8 narks won't beat his door in with sledge hammers, rush in waving their guns "WHATZAT YOU'RE SMOKING?" jerk the pipe out of his mouth and strip him naked. The permissive society is passing now laws forbidding four or more unrelated persons to live in the same dwelling. MOB of course assumes the right of any group of individuals to withdraw into communes of their choice quite simply to see people they want to look at and not have people they don't want to look at shoved at them night and day. These withdrawal units are called MOBS. The Hippies already operate MOBS. Many other MOBS are possible—MOBS emitting the same brain waves who can slow their pulses together, telepathic MOBS who never speak, MOBS dedicated to exploring space without an aqualung. And not necessarily impractical. Chairman Mao thinks "The real battle is inside our own skulls." Perhaps those who control inner space control outer space as well. Here is a cartoon strip encounter between the brain waves MOB and the narks . . . The narks burst through a door like King Kong gun out eyes wild . . . Four kids look at them with something too neutral to be called contempt. The kids slow down their hearts and lower blood pressure . . . an icy grey mist fills the room . . . The narks flee in terror . . . They are mowed down outside by cops with riot guns . . .

In view of the Tate murders attributed to a commune of Hippies known simply as the "Family" living in Death Valley,[80] we will make the MOB stand on criminals and criminal communes clear. A criminal is someone who commits crimes against property and crimes against persons. We feel that criminals are not minding their own business. Someone who steals your typewriter, starts barroom fights, kicks an old bum to death, is not minding his own business at all. The Thuggees of India, the Mafia, the Ku Klux Klan are examples of criminal communes. Strangling someone and stealing his money, throwing acid in his face, lynching beating and burning people to death is not minding one's own business. The Tate murderers were not minding their own business any more than the Klan does. These may be communes but they are not MOBS. Criminal communes like the Mafia may exist in symbiosis with existing social orders. No criminal MOBS on a mass scale could render existing societies obsolete. Who would object to the formation of MOBS? Those who now hold a parasitic point of advantage at the expense of others. So the good guys separate out from the bad guys. And who are the good guys on this set? Nothing special just reasonably well intentioned persons. Doesn't necessarily run to the nearest police station if he smells pot out some one's window not looking to start any barroom fights or stomp any old bums just minding his own business and wishing others would do the same. And who are the bad guys? The bad guys are those who can't mind their own business because they have no business of their own to mind any more than a small pox virus. Their business is degrading, harassing and frightening other people. The hard core opposition consists of those who could find no business of their own to mind even if they were given the opportunity to do so . . .

"What are you going to do Joe?" says one nark to another.

A smile lights up Joe's face the way it does when he busts a sick junky across his false teeth.

"I'm going fishing."

"We're coming with you."

The Supervisor screams after them: "You jokers think you can walk out on the United States of America? And that's a Federal question!"

They don't answer the Federal question. They are going to join a fishing MOB.

The MOBS gain an advantage by being exactly who and where they are . . . emitting the same brain waves . . .

"It was like a wall sir. It *stopped* us sir. It was most unnerving sir."

"I'm sure it was, Clancy" said the Chief wearily. "You may go." It was the third search party he had sent out in the past week against Commune 23. They had all come back with this talk of a wall. The Chief mixed himself a Scotch . . ." *Brain wave control* . . . We can't even reach them on a *physical* level . . . Why this is evil incarnate . . . Absolutely no way of knowing what they are doing in there . . . Well what is it Clancy?"

"I'm leaving you sir . . . You see I always hada mind to raise ferrets . . . It was that put me onto police work in the first place sir them ferrets going down rat holes sir I thought of criminals as rats sir and myself as a righteous ferret sir . . . I'm going to join a ferret MOB sir and raise ferrets . . ."

And criminals are defecting to the MOBS in droves. The crime statistics sag ominously. Sad old turnkeys mutter through empty cells. Desperate for arrests police prowl the streets like paranoid dogs. And some of the cold grey narks explode from altered pressure like a deep sea creature brought up from the depths.

A world wide reaction comparable to the reaction that crushed the liberal movements of 1848 is now under weigh.[81]

On one side we have MOBS dedicated to minding their own business without interference. On the other side we have the enemies of MOB dedicated to interference. Equipped with new techniques of computerized thought control the enemies of MOB could inflict a permanent defeat. MOB want to know just where everybody stands. Wouldn't advise you to try sitting on that fence. It's electric.

Your enemies then are the enemies of MOB. You can do more to destroy these enemies with tape recorders and video cameras than you can with machine guns. Video tape puts any number of machine guns into your hands. However, it is difficult to convince a revolutionary that this weapon is actually more potent than gelignite or guns. What do revolutionaries want? Vengeance, or a real change? Both perhaps. It is difficult for those who have suffered outrageous brutality and oppression to forget about vengeance, which is why I postulated the wholesome catharsis of MA. Actually MA is the Mass Assassination of enemy word and image. And this brings us to a basic question that every revolutionary must ask himself. Can I live without enemies? Can any human being live without enemies? No human being has ever done so yet. If the present revolutionary movement is to amount to more than a change of management, presenting the same old good-guy, bad-guy movie, a basic change of consciousness must take place. Now I will discuss some procedures which are also weapons, and very potent weapons, which also involve such a change of consciousness.

In *The Invisible Generation*,[82] first published in IT and in the *Los Angeles Free Press* in 1966 and reprinted in *The Job*, I consider the potential of thousands of people with recorders, portable and stationary, messages passed along like signal drums, a parody of the President's speech up and down tenement balconies, in and out open windows, through walls, over courtyards, taken up by barking dogs, muttering bums, music, traffic down windy streets, across parks and soccer fields. Illusion is a revolutionary weapon. To point out some specific uses of prerecorded, cutup tapes played back in the streets, as a revolutionary weapon.

*To spread rumors.*

Put 10 operators with carefully prepared recordings out at the rush hour and see how quick the word gets around. People don't know where they heard it, but they heard it.

*To discredit opponents.*

Take a recorded Wallace Speech, cut in stammering, coughs, sneezes, hiccups, snarls, pain screams, fear whimperings, apoplectic sputterings, slobbering, drooling idiot noises, sex and animal sound effects, and play it back in the streets, subways, stations, parks, political rallies.

*As a front line weapon to produce and escalate riots.*

There is nothing mystical about this operation. Riot sound effects can produce an actual riot in a riot situation. *Recorded police whistles will draw cops. Recorded gunshots, and their guns are out.*

*"MY GOD, THEY'RE KILLING US."*

A guardsman said later: "I heard the shots and saw my buddy go down, his face covered in blood" (turned out he'd been hit by a stone from a sling shot) and I thought, well, this is it."

BLOODY WEDNESDAY.[83] A DAZED AMERICA COUNTED 23 DEAD AND 32 WOUNDED, 6 CRITICALLY.

Here's a run of the mill, pre-riot situation. Protestors have been urged to demonstrate peacefully; police and guardsmen to exercise restraint. Ten tape recorder operators on set, hidden recorders strapped under their coats, play back and record control from lapel buttons. They have prerecorded riot sound effects from Chicago, Paris, Mexico City, Kent, Ohio.[84] If they adjust sound level of recordings to surrounding sound levels they will not be detected. Police scuffle with a demonstrator.[85] The operators converge. Turn on Chicago, record, play back, move on to the next scuffles, record, play back, keep moving. Things are hotting up, a cop is down groaning. Shrill chorus of recorded pig squeals and parody groans.

Could you cool a riot by recording the calmest cop and the most reasonable demonstrators? Maybe! However, it's a lot easier to start trouble than stop it. Just pointing out that cutups on the tape recorder can be used as a weapon. You'll observe that the operators are making a cutup as they go. They're cutting in Chicago, Paris, Mexico City, Kent, Ohio with the present sound effects at random, and that is a cutup.

*As a long range weapon to scramble and nullify associational alliances*[86] *put down by mass media.*

The control of the mass media depends on laying down lines of association. When the lines are cut the associational connections are broken.

"President Johnson burst into a swank apartment and held 3 maids at gunpoint 26 miles north of Saigon yesterday."[87]

You can cut the mutter line of the mass media and put the altered mutter line out in the streets with a tape recorder. Consider the mutter line of the daily press. It goes up with the morning papers, millions of people reading the same words, belching, chewing, swearing, chuckling, reacting to the same words. In different ways, of course. "A motion praising Mr. Callaghan's[88] action in banning the South African Cricket Tour has spoiled the colonel's breakfast."[89] All reacting one way or another to the paper world of unseen events which becomes an integral part of your reality. You will notice that this process is continually subject to random juxtaposition. Just what sign did you see in the Green Park station as you glanced up from *The People*? Just who called as you were reading your letter in *The Times*? What were you reading when your wife broke a dish in the kitchen? An unreal paper world and yet completely real because it is *actually* happening. Mutter line of the Evening News,

TV. Fix yourself on millions of people all watching "Jessie James" or "The Virginian" at the same time. International mutter line of the weekly news magazines[90] always dated a week ahead. Have you noticed it's the kiss of death to be on the front cover of *Time*? Madame Nhu[91] was there when her husband was killed and her government fell. Verwoerd[92] was on the front cover of *Time* when a demon tapeworm gave the order for his death through a messenger of the same. Read the Bible, kept to himself, no bad habits, you know the type: Ol' reliable. *Read all about it.*

So stir in news stories, TV plays, stock market quotations, adverts, and put the altered mutter line out in the street.

The underground press serves as the only effective counter to a growing power and more sophisticated techniques used by establishment mass media to falsify, misrepresent, misquote, rule out of consideration as *a priori* ridiculous or simply ignore and block out of existence data, books, discoveries that they consider prejudicial to establishment interest.

I suggest that the underground press could perform this function much more effectively by the use of cutup techniques. For example, prepare cutups of the ugliest reactionary statements you can find and surround them with the ugliest pictures. Now give it the drool, slobber animal, noise treatment and put it out on the mutter line with recorders. Run a scramble[93] page in every issue of transcribed tape recorder cutup of news, radio, and TV. Put the recordings out on the mutter line before the paper hits the stands. It gives you a funny feeling to see a headline that's been going around and around in your head. The underground press could add a mutter line to their adverts and provide a unique advertising service. Cut the product in with pop tunes, cut the product in with advertising slogans and jingles of other products and siphon off the sales. Anybody who doubts that these techniques work has only to put them to the test. The techniques here described are in use by the CIA and agents of other countries. Ten years ago they were making systematic street recordings in every district of Paris. I recall the

Voice of America[94] man in Tangier and a room full of tape recorders and you could hear some strange sounds through the wall. Kept to himself, "hello" in the hall. Nobody was ever allowed in that room, not even a Fatimah.[95] Of course, there are many technical elaborations like long-range directional mics. When you cut the prayer call in with hog grunts it doesn't pay to be walking around the market with a portable tape recorder.[96]

An article in *New Scientist* June 4, 1970, page 470, entitled "Electronic Arts of Noncommunication" by Richard C. French[97] gives the clue for more precise technical instructions.

In 1968, with the help of Ian Sommerville and Anthony Balch,[98] I took a short passage of my recorded voice and cut it into intervals of one twenty-fourth of a second on movie tape—(movie tape is larger and easier to splice)—and rearranged the order of the 24th second intervals of recorded speech. The original words are quite unintelligible but new words emerge. The voice is still there and you can immediately recognize the speaker. Also the tone of voice remains. If the tone is friendly, hostile, sexual, poetic, sarcastic, lifeless, despairing, this will be apparent in the altered sequence.

I did not realize at the time that I was using a technique that has been in existence since 1881 . . . I quote from Mr. French's article . . . "Designs for speech scramblers go back to 1881 and the desire to make telephone and radio communications unintelligible to third parties has been with us ever since" . . . The message is scrambled in transmission and then unscrambled at the other end. There are many of these speech scrambling devices that work on different principles . . ." Another device which saw service during the war was the time division scrambler. The signal is chopped up into elements .005 cm[99] long. These elements are taken in groups or frames and rearranged in a new sequence. Imagine that the speech recorded is recorded on magnetic tape which is cut into pieces .02 long and the pieces rearranged into a new sequence. This can actually be done and gives a good idea what speech sounds like when scrambled in this way." This I had done in 1968. And this is an extension of the cutup method. The simplest cutup cuts a page down the middle and across the middle into four sections. Section 1 is then placed with section 4 and section 3 with section 2 in a new sequence. Carried further we can break the page down into smaller and smaller units in altered sequences.

The original purpose of scrambling devices was to make the message unintelligible without the unscrambling code. Another use for speech scramblers could be to impose thought control on a mass scale. Consider the human body and nervous system as unscrambling devices. A common virus like the cold sore could sensitize the subject to unscramble messages. Drugs like LSD and Dim-N$^{100}$ could also act as unscrambling devices. Moreover, the mass media could sensitize millions of people to receive scrambled versions of the same set of data. Remember that when the human nervous system unscrambles a scrambled message this will seem to the subject like his very own ideas which just occurred to him, which indeed it did.

Take a card, any card. In most cases he will not suspect its extraneous origin. That is the run of the mill newspaper reader who receives the scrambled message uncritically and assumes that it reflects his own opinions independently arrived at. On the other hand, the subject may recognize or suspect the extraneous origin of voices that are literally hatching out in his head. Then we have the classic syndrome of paranoid psychosis. Subject hears voices. Anyone can be made to hear voices with scrambling techniques. It is not difficult to expose him to the actual scrambled message, any part of which can be made intelligible. This can be done with street recorders, recorders in cars, doctored radio and TV sets. In his own flat if possible, if not in some bar or restaurant he frequents. If he doesn't talk to himself, he soon will do. You bug his flat. Now he is really round the bend hearing his own voice out of radio and TV broadcasts and the conversation of passing strangers. See how easy it is? Remember the scrambled message is partially unintelligible and in any case he gets the tone. Hostile white voices unscrambled by a Negro will also activate by association every occasion on which he has been threatened or humiliated by whites. To carry it further you can use recordings of voices known to him. You can turn him against his friends by hostile scrambled messages in a friend's voice. This will activate all his disagreements with that friend. You can condition him to like his enemies by friendly scrambled messages in enemy voices. On the other hand the voices can be friendly and reassuring. He is now working for the CIA, the GPU,[101] or whatever, and these are his orders. They now have an agent who has no information to give away and who doesn't have to be paid. And he is now completely under control. If he doesn't obey orders they can give him the hostile voice treatment. No, "They" are not God or super technicians from outer space. Just technicians operating with well-known equipment and using techniques that can be duplicated by anyone else who can buy and operate this equipment.

To see how scrambling technique could work on a mass scale, imagine that a news magazine like *Time* got out a whole issue a week before publication and filled it with news based on predictions following a certain line, without attempting the impossible, giving our boys a boost in every story and the Commies as many defeats and casualties as possible, a whole issue of *Time* formed from slanted prediction of future news. Now imagine this scrambled out through the mass media.

With minimal equipment you can do the same thing on a smaller scale. You need a scrambling device, TV, radio, two video cameras, a ham radio station and a simple photo studio with a few props and actors. For a start you scramble the news all together and spit it out every which way on ham radio and street recorders. You construct fake news broadcasts on video camera. For the pictures you can use mostly old footage. Mexico City will do for a riot in Saigon and vice versa. For a riot in Santiago Chile you can use the Londonderry pictures. Nobody knows the difference. Fires, earthquakes, plane crashes can be moved around. For example, here is a plane crash, 112 dead north of Barcelona and here is a plane crash in Toronto 108 dead. So move the picture of the Barcelona plane crash over to Toronto and Toronto to Barcelona. And you scramble your fabricated news in with actual news broadcasts. You have an advantage which your opposing player does not have. He must conceal his manipulations. You are under no such necessity. In fact you can advertise the fact that you are writing news in advance and trying to make it happen by techniques which anybody can use. And that makes you NEWS. And a TV personality as well, if you play it right. You want the widest possible circulation for your cutup video tapes. Cutup techniques could swamp the mass media with total illusion.

Fictional dailies retroactively cancelled the San Francisco earthquake and the Halifax explosion[102] as journalistic hoaxes, and doubt released from the skin law extendable and ravenous, consumed all the facts of history.

Mr. French concludes his article . . . "The use of modern microelectric integrated circuits could lower the cost of speech scramblers enough to see them in use by private citizens. Codes and ciphers have always had a strong appeal to most people and I think scramblers will as well . . ."

It is generally assumed that speech must be consciously understood to cause an effect. Early experiments with subliminal images have shown that this is not true. A number of research projects could be based on speech scramblers. We have all seen the experiment where someone speaking hears his own recorded voice back a few seconds later. Soon he cannot go on talking. Would scrambled speech have the same effect? To what extent are scrambled messages actually unscrambled by experimental subjects? To what extent does a language act as an unscrambling device, western languages tending to unscramble in either-or conflict terms? To what extent does the tone of voice used by a speaker impose a certain unscrambling sequence on the listener?

Many of the cutup tapes would be entertaining and in fact entertainment is the most promising field for cutup techniques. Imagine a pop festival like Phun City scheduled for July 24th, 25th, 26th, 1970 at Ecclesden Common, Patching, near Worthing, Sussex, Festival[103] area comprised of car park and camping area, a rock auditorium, a village with booths and cinema, a large wooded area. A number of tape recorders are planted in the woods and the village. As many as possible so as to lay down a grid of sound over the whole festival. Recorders have tapes of pre-recorded material, music, news broadcasts, recordings from other festivals, etc. At all times some of the recorders are playing back and some are recording. The recorders recording at any time are of course recording the crowd and the other tape recorders that are playing back at varying distances. This cuts in the crowd who will be hearing their own voices back. Play back, wind back and record could be electronically controlled with varying intervals. Or they could be hand operated, the operator deciding what intervals of play back, record, and wind back to use. Effect is greatly increased by a large number of festival goers with portable recorders playing back and recording as they walk around the festival. We can carry it further with projection screens and video cameras. Some of the material projected is pre-prepared, sex films, films of other festivals, and this material is cut in with live TV broadcasts and shots of the crowd. Of course, the rock festival will be cut in on the screens, thousands of fans with portable recorders recording and playing back, the singer could direct play back and record. Set up an area for travelling performers, jugglers, animal acts, snake charmers, singers, musicians, and cut these acts in. Film and tape from the festival, edited for the best material, could then be used at other festivals.

Quite a lot of equipment and engineering to set it up. The festival could certainly be enhanced if as many festival goers as possible bring portable tape recorders to record and play back at the festival.

Any message, music, conversation you want to pass around, bring it pre-recorded on tape so everybody takes a piece of your tape home.[104]

Research project: to find out to what extent scrambled messages are unscrambled, that is scanned out by experimental subjects. The simplest experiment consists in playing back a scrambled message to subject. Message could contain simple commands. Does the scrambled message have any command value comparable to post-hypnotic suggestion? Is the actual content of the message received? What drugs, if any, increase the ability to unscramble messages? Do subjects vary widely in this ability? Are the scrambled messages in the subjects' own voice more effective than messages in other voices? Are messages scrambled in certain voices more easily unscrambled by specific subjects? Is the message more potent with both word and image scrambled on video tape? Now to use for example a video-tape message with a unified emotional content. Let us say the message is fear. For this we take all the past fear shots of the subject we can collect or evoke. We cut these in with fear words and pictures, with threats, etc. This is all acted out and would be upsetting enough in any case. Now let's try it scrambled and see if we get an even stronger effect. The subject's blood pressure, rate of heartbeat, and brainwaves are recorded as we play back the scrambled tape. His face is photographed and visible to him on video camera at all times. The actual scrambling with tape can be done in two ways. It can be a completely random operation like pulling pieces out of a hat and if this is done several consecutive units may occur together, yielding an identifiable picture or an intelligible word. Both methods of course can be used at varying intervals. Blood pressure, heartbeat, and brain-wave recordings will show the operator what material is producing the strongest reaction and he will of course zero in. And remember the subject can see his face at all times and his face is being photographed. As the Peeping Tom said, "the most frightening thing is fear in your own face." If the subject becomes too disturbed, we have peace and safety tapes ready.

Now here is a sex tape: this consists of a sex scene acted out by the ideal sexual object of the subject and his ideal self image. Shown straight it might be exciting enough, now scramble it. It takes a few seconds for scrambled tapes to hatch out, and then, can scrambled sex tapes zeroing in on the subject's reactions and brain waves result in spontaneous orgasm? Can this be extended to other functions of the body? A mic secreted in the watercloset and all his shits and farts recorded and scrambled in with stern nanny voices commanding him to shit, and the young liberal MP shits in his pants on the platform right under Old Glory. Could laugh tapes, sneeze tapes, hiccup tapes, cough tapes, give rise to laughing, sneezing, hiccupping, and coughing?

To what extent can physical illness be induced by scrambled illness tapes? We take, for example, a sound and color picture of subject with a cold. Later, when subject is fully recovered, we take color and sound film of recovered subject. We now scramble the cold pictures and sound track in with present sound and image track. We also *project* the cold pictures on present pictures. Now we try using some of Mr. Hubbard's Reactive Mind phrases which are supposed in themselves to produce illness. *To be me, To be you, To stay here, To stay there, To be a body, To be bodies, To stay present, To stay absent.*[105] Well we scramble all this in together and show it to the subject. Could seeing and hearing this sound and image track, scrambled down to *very* small units, bring about an attack of cold virus? If such a cold tape does actually produce an attack of cold virus we cannot say that we have created a virus, perhaps we have merely activated a latent virus. Many viruses as you know are latent in the body and may be activated. We can try the same with a cold sore, with hepatitis, always remembering that we may be activating a latent virus and in no sense creating a laboratory virus. However, we may be in a position to do this. Is a virus perhaps simply very small units of sound and image? Remember the only image a virus has is the image and soundtrack it can impose on you. The yellow eyes of jaundice, the pustules of smallpox, etc. impose on you against your will. The same is certainly true of scrambled word and image. Its existence *is* the word and image it can make you unscrambled. *Take a card, any card.* This does not mean that it is actually a virus. Perhaps to construct a laboratory virus we would need both camera and sound crew and a biochemist as well. I quote from the *International Paris Tribune* an article on the synthetic gene, Dr. Har Gobin Korana[106] had made a gene synthetically.

"It is the beginning of the end."

This was the immediate reaction to this news from the science attaché at one of Washington's major embassies. "If you can make genes you can eventually make new viruses for which there are no cures. Any little country with good biochemists could make such biological weapons. It would take only a small laboratory. If it can be done, somebody will do it." For example, a death virus could be created that carries the coded message of death. A death tape, in fact. No doubt the technical details are complex and perhaps a team of sound and cameramen working with biochemists would give us the answer.

And now the question as to whether scrambling techniques could be used to spread healthful and pleasant messages. Perhaps. On the other hand the scrambled words and tape act like a virus in that they force something on the subject against his will. More to the point would be to discover how the old scanning patterns could be altered so that the subject liberates his own spontaneous scanning pattern. Quote from article in *New Scientist*:[107] *New Scientist* 2 July, 1970 . . . Current memory theory posits a seven second temporary "buffer store" preceding the main one: a blow on the head wipes out memory of this much prior time because it erases the contents of the buffer. Daedalus[108] observes that the sense of the present also covers just this range and so suggests that our sensory input is in effect recorded on an endless time loop, providing some seven seconds of delay for scanning before erasure. In this time the brain edits, makes sense of, and selects for storage key features. The weird *déjà vu* sensation that "now" has happened before is clearly due to brief erasure failure, so that we encounter already stored memory data coming round again. Time dragging or racing must reflect tape speed.[109]

A simple experiment will demonstrate this erasure process in operation. Making street recordings and playing them back, you will hear things you *do not* remember, sometimes said in a loud clear voice, must have been quite close to you, nor do you necessarily remember them when you *hear* the recording back. The sound has been erased according to a scanning pattern which is automatic.

This means that what you notice and store as memory as you walk down a street is scanned out of a much larger selection of data which is then erased from the memory. For the walker then, signs he has passed and people he has passed are erased from his mind and cease to exist for him.[110] Now to make this scanning process conscious and controllable, try this:

Walk down a city block with a camera and take what you notice, moving the camera around as closely as possible to follow the direction of your eyes. The point is to make the camera your eyes and take what your eyes are scanning out of the larger picture. At the same time take the street at wide angle from a series of still positions. The street of the operator is, of course, the street as seen by the operator. It is of course different from the street seen at wide angle. Much of it is in fact missing. Now you can make arbitrary scanning patterns—that is cover first one side of the street and then the other in accordance with a preconceived plan. So you are breaking down the automatic scanning patterns. You could also make a color scanning pattern; that is, scan out green, blue, red, etc. insofar as you can with your camera. That is, you are using an arbitrary preconceived scanning pattern, in order to break down automatic scanning patterns. A number of operators do this and then scramble in their tapes together and with wide angle tapes. This could train a subject to see at a wider angle and also to ignore and erase at will. Now all this is readily subject to experimental verification on control subjects. Nor need the equipment be all that complicated. I have shown how it could work with feedback from brainwaves and visceral response and videotape photos of subject taken while he is seeing and hearing the tape, simply to show optimum effectiveness. You can start with two tape recorders. The simplest scrambling device is scissors and splicing equipment. You can start scrambling words, make any kind of tapes and scramble them and observe the effects on friends and on yourself. Next step is sound film and then video camera. Of course results from individual experiments could lead to mass experiments, mass fear tapes, riot tapes, etc. The possibilities here for research and experiment are virtually unlimited and I have simply made a few very simple suggestions.

"A virus is characterized and limited by obligate cellular parasitism. All viruses must parasitize living cells for their replication. For all viruses the infection cycle comprises entry into the host, intracellular replication, and escape from the body of the host to initiate a new cycle in a fresh host." I am quoting here from *Mechanisms of Virus Infection* edited by Dr. Wilson Smith.[111] "In its wild state the virus has not proved to be a very adaptable organism. Some viruses have burned themselves out since they were 100 per cent fatal and there were no reservoirs. "Each strain of virus is rigidly programmed for a certain attack on certain tissues. If the attack fails, the virus does not gain entry and cannot carry on its life cycle of entry replication and escape to infect a new host. There are of course the virus mutations, and the influenza virus has proved quite versatile in this way."[112]

Generally it's the simple repetition of the same method of entry, and if that method is blocked by any body or other agency such as interferon, the attack fails. By and large our virus is a stupid organism. Now we can think for the virus, devise a number of alternate methods of entry. For example, the host is simultaneously attacked by an ally virus who tells him that everything is alright and by a pain and fear virus. So the virus is now using an old method of entry, namely the tough cop and the con cop.

We have considered the possibility that a virus *is* the very small units of sound and image. So conceived the virus can be made to order in the laboratory. Ah, but for the tapes to be effective you must have also the actual virus and what is this so actual virus? New viruses turn up from time to time. From where do they turn up? Well, let's see how we can *make* a virus turn up. We plot now our virus and its symptoms and make a scrambled tape. Some subjects will be more susceptible than others to this tape. The most susceptible, that is those who reproduce some of the desired symptoms, will then be scrambled into more tapes until we scramble our virus into existence. This birth of a virus occurs when our virus is able to reproduce itself in a host and pass itself on to another host. Perhaps too, with the virus under laboratory control it can be tamed for useful purposes.

Now imagine for example, a sex virus. It so inflames the sex centers in the back brain that the host is driven mad from sexuality, all other considerations are blacked out. Parks full of naked, frenzied people, shitting, pissing, ejaculating, and screaming. So the virus could be malignant, blacking out all regulations and end in exhaustion, convulsions, and death.

Now let us attempt the same thing with tape. We organize a sex-tape festival. 100,000 people bring their scrambled sex tapes, and video tapes as well, to scramble in together. Projected on vast screens, muttering out over the crowd, sometimes it slows down so you see a few seconds, then scrambled again, and slow down, scramble. Soon it will scramble them all naked. The cops and the National Guard are stripping down. LET'S GET OURSELVES SOME CIV-VIES. Now a thing like that could be messy, but those who survive it recover from the madness. Or, say a small select group of really like-minded people get together with their sex tapes, you see the process is now being brought under control. And the fact that anybody can do it is in itself a limiting factor.

Here is Mr. Hart,[113] who wants to infect everyone with his own image and turn them all into himself, so he scrambles himself and dumps himself out in search of worthy vessels. If nobody else knows about scrambling techniques he might scramble himself quite a stable of replicas. But anybody can do it. So go on, scramble your sex words out, and find suitable mates.

If you want to, scramble yourself out there, every stale joke, fart, chew, sneeze, and stomach grumble. If your trick no work you better run. Everybody doing it, they all scramble in together and the population of the earth just settles down to a nice even brown color. Scrambles is the *democratic* way, the way of full cellular representation. Scrambles is the *American* way.[114]

I have suggested that virus can be created to order in the laboratory from very small units of sound and image. Such a preparation is not in itself biologically active but it could activate or even create virus in susceptible subjects. A carefully prepared jaundice tape could activate or create the jaundice virus in liver cells, especially in cases where the liver is already damaged. The operator is in effect directing a virus revolution of the cells. Since DOR seems to attack those exposed to it at the weakest point, release of this force could coincide with virus attack. Reactive Mind phrases could serve the same purpose of rendering subjects more susceptible to virus attack.

It will be seen that scrambled speech already has many of the characteristics of virus. When the speech takes and unscrambles, this occurs compulsively and against the will of the subject. A virus must remind you of its presence. Whether it is the nag of a cold sore or the torturing spasms of rabies the virus reminds you of its unwanted presence. "HERE ME IS."

So does scrambled word and image. The units are unscrambling compulsively, presenting certain words and images to the subject and this repetitive presentation is irritating certain bodily and neutral areas. The cells so irritated can produce over a period of time the biologic virus units. We now have a new virus that can be communicated and indeed the subject may be desperate to communicate this thing that is bursting inside him. He is heavy with the load. Could this load be good and beautiful? Is it possible to create a virus which will communicate calm and sweet reasonableness? A virus must parasitize a host in order to survive. It uses the cellular material of the host to make copies of itself. In most cases this is damaging to the host. The virus gains entrance by fraud and maintains itself by force. An unwanted guest who makes you sick to look at is never good or beautiful. It is moreover a guest who always repeats itself word for word take for take.

Remember the life cycle of a virus . . . penetration of a cell or activation within the cell, replication within the cell, escape from cell to invade other cells, escape from host to infect a new host. This infection can take place in many ways and those who find themselves heavy with the load of a new virus generally use a shotgun technique to cover a wide range of infection routes . . . cough, sneeze, spit and fart at every opportunity. Save shit, piss, snot, scabs, sweat stained clothes and all bodily secretions for dehydration. The composite dust can be unobtrusively billowed out a roach bellows in subways, dropped from windows in bags, or sprayed out a crop duster . . . Carry with you at all times an assortment of vectors . . . lice, fleas, bed bugs, and little aviaries of mosquitoes and biting flies filled with your blood . . . I see no beauty in that.

There is only one case of a favorable virus influence ben-
efiting an obscure species of Australian mice. On the other
hand, if a virus produces no damaging symptoms we have
no way of ascertaining its existence and this happens with
latent virus infections. It has been suggested that yellow
races resulted from a jaundice-like virus which produced a
permanent mutation not necessarily damaging, which was
passed along genetically. The same may be true of the word.
The word itself may be a virus that has achieved a permanent status with the host. However, no known virus in existence at the present time acts in this manner, so the question
of a beneficent virus remains open. It seems advisable to
concentrate on a general defense against all virus.[115]

Mr. L. Ron Hubbard, the founder of Scientology, says
that certain words and word combinations can produce serious illnesses and mental disturbances. I can claim some skill
in the scrivener's trade, but I cannot *guarantee* to write a passage that will make someone physically ill. If Mr. Hubbard's
claim is justified, it is certainly a matter for further research,
and we can easily find out experimentally whether his claim
is justified or not. Mr. Hubbard bases the power he attributes
to words on his theory of engrams. An engram is defined as
word, sound, image recorded by the subject in a period of
pain and unconsciousness. Some of this material may be reassuring: I think he's going to be alright. Reassuring material is
an ally engram and ally engrams, according to Mr. Hubbard,
are just as abberative as hostile or pain engrams. Any part
of this recording played back to the subject later will reactivate operation pain, he may actually develop a headache
and feel depressed, anxious, or tense. Well, Mr. Hubbard's
engram theory is very easily subject to experimental verification. Take ten volunteer subjects, subject them to a pain
or stimulus accompanied by certain words and sounds and
images. You can in fact act out little skits.
    "Quickly nurse, before I lose my little nigger," bellows a
southern surgeon, and now a beefy white hand falls on the

fragile black shoulder. "Yes, he's gonna be alright, he's gonna pull through."

*"If I had my way I'd let these animals die on the operating table."*

"You do not have your way, you have your duty as a doctor, we must do everything in our power to save human lives." And so forth.

It's the tough cop and the con cop. The ally engram is ineffective without the pain engram, just as the con cop's arm around your shoulder, his soft persuasive voice in your ear, are indeed sweet nothings without the tough cop's blackjack. Now to what extent can words recorded during medical unconsciousness be recalled through hypnosis or scientological processing? To what extent does the playback of this material affect the subject unpleasantly? Is this effect enhanced by scrambling the material, pain and ally, at very short intervals? It would seem that a scrambled engram's picture could almost dump an operating scene right in the subject's lap. Mr. Hubbard has charted his version of what he calls the Reactive Mind. This is roughly similar to Freud's id, a sort of built-in self defeating mechanism. As set forth by Mr. Hubbard this consists of a number of quite ordinary phrases. He claims that reading these phrases, or hearing them spoken, can cause illness, and gives this as his reason for not publishing this material. Is he perhaps saying these are magic words? Spells, in fact? If so they could be quite a weapon scrambled up with imaginative sound- and image-track. Here now is the magic that turns men into swine. To be an *animal*: a lone pig grunts, shits, squeals and slobbers down garbage. To be *animals*: Now a chorus of a thousand pigs. Cut that in with videotape police pictures and play it back to them and see if you get a reaction from this so Reactive Mind.

Now here's another.[116] To be a body, well let's show an attractive body, to rope the marks in. And a nice body symphony to go with it, rhythmic heart beats, contented stomach grumblings. To be bodies: recordings and pictures of hideous, aged, diseased bodies farting, pissing, shitting, groaning, dying. *To do everything*: man in a filthy apartment surrounded by unpaid bills, unanswered letters, jumps up and starts washing dishes and writing letters. *To do nothing*: he slumps in a chair, jumps up, slumps in chair, jumps up. Finally slumps in the chair, drooling in idiot helplessness, while he looks at the disorder piled around him. The Reactive Mind commands could also be used to advantage with illness tapes. While projecting past coldsore onto the subject's face, or playing back to him a past illness tape, you can say: to be me, to be you, to stay here, to stay there, to be a body, to be bodies, to stay in, to stay out, to stay present, to stay absent. To what extent are these Reactive Mind phrases when scrambled effective in causing disagreeable symptoms in control volunteer subjects? As to Mr. Hubbard's claims for the Reactive Mind, only research can give us the answers.[117]

The RM then is an artifact designed to limit and stultify on a mass scale. In order to have this effect it must be widely implanted. This can readily be done with modern electronic equipment and the techniques described in this treatise. The RM consists of commands which seem harmless and in fact unavoidable . . . To be a body . . . but which can have the most horrific consequences.

Here are some sample RM screen effects . . .

As the theater darkens a bright light appears on the left side of the screen. The screen lights up

To be nobody . . . On screen shadow of ladder and soldier incinerated by the Hiroshima blast

To be everybody . . . Street crowds, riots, panics

To be me . . . A beautiful girl and a handsome young man point to selves

To be you . . . They point to audience . . .

Hideous hags and old men, lepers, drooling idiots point to themselves and to the audience as they intone . . .

To be me

To be you

Command no. 5 . . . To be myself

Command no. 6 . . . To be others

On screen a narcotics officer is addressing an audience of school boys. Spread out on a table in front of him are syringes, kief pipes, samples of heroin, hashish, LSD.

Officer: "Five trips on a drug can be a pleasant and exciting experience . . ."

On screen young trippers . . . "I'm really myself for the first time"

ETC[118] happy trips . . . To be myself . . . no. 5 . . .

Officer: "THE SIXTH WILL PROBABLY BLOW YOUR HEAD OFF"

Shot shows a man blowing his head off with a shotgun in his mouth . . .

Officer: "Like a 15 year old boy I knew until recently, you could well end up dying in your own spew . . . To be others . . . no. 6 . . .

To be an animal . . . A lone Wolf Scout . . .

To be animals: He joins other wolf scouts playing, laughing, shouting

To be an animal . . . Bestial and ugly human behavior . . . brawls, disgusting eating and sex scenes

To be animals . . . Cows, sheep and pigs driven to the slaughter house

To be a body

To be bodies

A beautiful body . . . a copulating couple . . . Cut back and forth and run on seven second loop for several minutes . . . scramble at different speeds . . . Audience must be made to realize that to be a body is to be bodies . . . A body only exists to be other bodies.

To be a body . . . Death scenes and recordings . . . a scramble of last words

To be bodies . . . Vista of cemeteries . . .

To do it now . . . Couple embracing hotter and hotter

To do it now . . . A condemned cell . . . Condemned man is same actor as lover . . . He is led away by the guards screaming and struggling. Cut back and forth between sex scene and man led to execution. Couple in sex scene have orgasm as the condemned man is hanged, electrocuted, gassed, garrotted, shot in the head with a pistol

To do it later . . . The couple pull away . . . One wants to go out and eat and go to a show or something . . . They put on their hats . . .

To do it later . . . Warder arrives at condemned cell to tell the prisoner he has a stay of execution

To do it now . . . Grim faces in the Pentagon. Strategic is on its way . . . Well THIS IS IT . . .

This sequence cut in with sex scenes and a condemned man led to execution, culminates in execution, orgasm, nuclear explosion . . . The condemned lover is a horribly burned survivor

To do it later . . . 1920 walk out sequence to "The Sunny Side of the Street"[119] . . . A disappointed general turns from the phone to say the President has opened top level hot wire talks with Russia and China . . . Condemned man gets another stay of execution

To be an animal . . . One lemming busily eating lichen . . .

To be animals . . . Hordes of lemmings swarming all over each other in mounting hysteria . . . A pile of drowned lemmings in front of somebody's nice little cottage on a Finnish lake where he is methodically going through sex positions with his girl friend. They wake up in a stink of dead lemmings

To be an animal . . . Little boy put on pot

To be animals . . . The helpless shitting infant is eaten alive by rats

To stay up . . . A man has just been hanged. The doctor steps forward with a stethoscope

To stay down . . . Body is carried out with the rope around neck . . . naked corpse on the autopsy table . . . corpse buried in quick lime

To stay up . . . Erect phallus

To stay down . . . White man burns off a Negro's genitals with blow torch . . . Theater darkens into the blow torch on left side of the screen

To stay present
To stay absent
To stay present . . . A boy masturbates in front of sex pictures . . . Cut to face of white man who is burning off black genitals with blow torch
To stay absent . . . Sex phantasies of the boy . . . The black slumps dead with genitals burned off and intestines popping out
To stay present . . . Boy watches strip tease, intent, fascinated . . . A man stands on trap about to be hanged
To stay present . . . Sex fantasies of the boy . . . "I pronounce this man dead."
To stay present . . . Boy whistles at girl in street . . . A man's body twists in the electric chair, his leg hairs crackling with blue fire
To stay absent . . . Boy sees himself in bed with girl . . . Man slumps dead in chair smoke curling from under the hood saliva dripping from his mouth . . .
The Theater lights up. In the sky a plane over Hiroshima . . . Little Boy slides out
To stay present . . .
The plane, the pilot, the American flag . . .
To stay absent . . . Theater darkens into atomic blast on screen
Here we see ordinary men and women going about their ordinary everyday jobs and diversions . . . subways, streets, buses, trains, airports, stations, waiting rooms, homes, flats, restaurants, offices, factories . . . working, eating, playing, defecating, making love
A chorus of voices cuts in RM phrases
To stay up
To stay down
Elevators, airports, stairs, ladders
To stay in
To stay out

Street signs, door signs, people at head of lines admitted to restaurants and theaters

To be myself

To be others

Customs agents check passports, man identifies himself at bank to cash check

To stay present

To stay absent

People watching films, reading, looking at TV . . .

A composite of this sound and image track is now run on seven second loop without change for several minutes.

Now cut in the horror pictures

To stay up

To stay down

Elevators, airports, stairs, ladders, hangings, castrations

To stay in

To stay out

Door signs, operation scenes . . . doctor tosses bloody tonsils, adenoids, appendix into receptacle

To stay present

To stay absent

People watching film . . . ether mask, ether vertigo . . . triangles, spheres, rectangles, pyramids, prisms, coils go away and come in in regular sequence . . . a coil coming in, two coils coming in, three coils coming in . . . a coil going away, two coils going away, four going away

A coil straight ahead going away, two coils on the left and right going away, three coils left right and center going away, four coils right left center and behind going away

A coil coming, two coils coming in, three coils coming in, four coils coming in . . . spirals of light . . . round and round faster faster, baby eaten by rats, hangings, electrocutions, castrations . . .

The RM can be cut in with the most ordinary scenes covering the planet in a smog of fear . . .

The RM is a built-in electronic police force armed with hideous threats. You don't want to be a cute little wolf cub? Alright, cattle to the slaughter house meat on a hook.

Here is a nostalgic reconstruction of the old fashioned Mayan methods. The wrong kind of workers with wrong thoughts are tortured to death in rooms under the pyramid . . . A young worker has been given a powerful hallucigen[120] and sexual stimulant . . . Naked he is strapped down and skinned alive . . . The dark Gods of pain are surfacing from the immemorial filth of time . . . The Oaub Bird[121] stands there, screams washing through his wild blue eyes. Others are crabs from the waist up clicking their claws in ecstasy, they dance around and mimic the flayed man. The scribes are busy with sketches . . . Now he is strapped into a segmented copper centipede and placed gently on a bed of hot coals . . . Soon the priests will dig the soft meat from the shell with their golden claws . . . Here is another youth staked out on an ant hill honey smeared on his eyes and genitals . . . Others with heavy weights on their backs are slowly dragged through wooden troughs in which shards of obsidian have been driven . . . So the priests are the masters of pain and fear and death . . . To do right . . . To obey the priests . . . To do wrong? The priest's very presence and a few banal words . . .

The priests postulated and set up a hermetic universe of which they were the axiomatic controllers. In so doing they became Gods who controlled the known universe of the workers. They became Fear and Pain, Death and Time. By making opposition seemingly impossible they failed to make any provision for opposition. There is evidence that this control system broke down in some areas before the arrival of the White God[122] Stellae have been found defaced and overturned, mute evidence of a worker's revolution. How did this happen? The history of revolutionary movements shows that they are usually led by defectors from the ruling class. The Spanish rule in South America was overthrown by Spanish revolutionaries. The French were driven out of Algeria by Algerians educated in France. Perhaps one of the priest Gods defected and organized a worker's revolution . . .

The priest gods in the temple. They move very slowly, faces ravaged with age and disease. Parasitic worms infest their dead fibrous flesh. They are making calculations from the sacred books.

"400,000,000 years ago on this day a grievous thing happened . . ."[123] Limestone skulls rain in through the porticos. The Young Maize God[124] leads the workers as they storm the temple and drag the priests out. They build a huge brush fire, throw the priests in and then throw the sacred books in after them. Time buckles and bends. The old Gods, surfacing from the immemorial depths of time, burst in the sky . . . Mr. Hart stands there looking at the broken stellae . . . "How did this happen?"

His control system must be absolute and world wide. Because such a control system is even more vulnerable to attack from without than revolt from within . . . Here is Bishop Landa burning the sacred books.[125] To give you an idea as to what is happening, imagine our civilization invaded by louts from outer space . . .

"Get some bulldozers in here. Clear out all this crap . . ." The formulae of all the natural sciences, books, paintings, the lot, swept into a vast pile and burned. And that's it. No one ever heard of it . . .

Three codices survived the vandalism of Bishop Landa and these are burned around the edges. No way to know if we have here the sonnets of Shakespeare, the Mona Lisa or the remnants of a Sears Roebuck catalog after the old outhouse burned down in a brush fire.[126] A whole civilization went up in smoke . . .

When the Spaniards arrived, they found the Mayan aristocrats lolling in hammocks. Well, time to show them what is what. Five captured workers bound and stripped, are castrated on a tree stump, the bleeding, sobbing, screaming bodies thrown into a pile . . .

"And now get this through your gook nuts. We want to see a pile of gold that big and we want to see it pronto. The White God has spoken."[127]

Consider now the human voice as a weapon. To what extent can the unaided human voice duplicate effects that can be done with a tape recorder? Learning to speak with the mouth shut, thus displacing your speech, is fairly easy. You can also learn to talk backwards, which is fairly difficult. I've seen people who can repeat what you are saying after you and finish at the same time. This is a most disconcerting trick, particularly when practiced on a mass scale at a political rally. Is it possible to actually scramble speech? A far-reaching biologic weapon can be forged from a new language. In fact such a language already exists. It exists as Chinese, a total language closer to the multi-leveled structure of experience, to the script derived from hieroglyphs, more closely related to the objects and areas described. The equanimity of the Chinese is undoubtedly derived from their language being structured for greater sanity. And notice the Chinese, wherever they are, retain their written and spoken language, while other immigrant peoples will lose their language in two generations. The aim of this project is to build a language in which certain falsifications inherent in all existing Western languages will be made incapable of formulation. The following falsifications to be deleted from the proposed language.[128]

*The IS of identity.* You are an animal. You are a body. Now whatever you may be you are not an "animal," you are not a "body," because these are verbal labels. The IS of identity always carries the implication of that and nothing else, and it also carries the assignment of permanent condition. To stay that way. All name calling presupposes the IS of identity. This concept is unnecessary in a hieroglyphic language like ancient Egyptian and in fact frequently omitted. No need to say the sun IS in the sky, sun in sky suffices. The verb *to be* can easily be omitted from any language and the followers of Count Korgybski[129] have done this, eliminating the verb[130] *to be* in English. However, it is difficult to tidy up the English language by arbitrary exclusion of concepts which remain in force so long as the unchanged language is spoken.

*The definite article THE.* THE contains the implication of one and only: THE God, THE universe, THE way, THE right, THE wrong. If there is another, then THAT universe, THAT way is no longer THE universe, THE way. The definite article THE will be deleted and the indefinite article *A* will take its place.

*The whole concept of EITHER/OR.* Right or wrong, physical or mental, true or false, the whole concept of OR will be deleted from the language and replaced by juxtaposition, by AND.[131] This is done to some extent in any pictorial language where the two concepts stand literally side by side. These falsifications inherent in English and other Western Alphabetical languages give the Reactive Mind commands their overwhelming force in these languages. Consider the IS of identity. When I say *to be me, to be you, to be myself, to be others—whatever* I may be called upon to be or say that I am—I am not the verbal label "myself." I cannot be and am not the verbal label "myself." The word BE in English contains, as a virus contains, its precoded message of damage, the categorical imperative of permanent condition. To be a body, to be nothing else, to stay a body. To be an animal, to be nothing else, to stay an animal. If you see the relation of the I to the body, as the relation of a pilot to his ship, you see the full crippling force of the Reactive Mind command *to be a body.* Telling the pilot to be the plane, then who will pilot the plane?

The IS of identity, assigning a rigid and permanent status, was greatly reinforced by passport and customs[132] control that came in after World War I. Whatever you may be, you are not the verbal labels in your passport any more than you are the word "self." So you must be prepared to prove at all times that you are what you are *not*. Much of the force of the Reactive Mind also depends on the falsification inherent in the categorical definite article THE. *THE now, THE past, THE time, THE space, THE energy, THE matter, THE universe.* The[133] definite article THE contains the implication of no other. THE universe locks you in *THE,* and denies the possibility of any other. If other universes are possible then THE universe is no longer THE, it becomes A. The definite article THE in the proposed language is deleted and replaced by A. Many of the RM commands are in point of fact contradictory commands and a contradictory command gains its force from the Aristotelian concept of either/or. To do everything, to do nothing, to have everything, to have nothing, to do it all, to do not any, to stay up, to stay down, to stay in, to stay out, to stay present, to stay absent. These are in point of fact either/or propositions. To do nothing *or* everything, to have it all *or* not any, *to stay present or stay absent.* Either/or is more difficult to formulate in a written language where both alternatives are pictorially represented and can be deleted entirely from the spoken language. The whole Reactive Mind can be in fact reduced to three little words—to be "THE." That is to be what you are not, verbal formulations.

I have frequently spoken of word and image as viruses or as acting as viruses, and this is not an allegorical comparison. It will be seen that the falsifications in syllabic Western languages are in point of fact actual virus mechanisms. The IS of identity *is* in point of fact *the* virus mechanism. If we can infer purpose from behavior then the purpose of a virus is TO SURVIVE. To survive at any expense to the host invaded. To be an animal, to be a body. To be an animal body that the virus can invade. To be animals, to be bodies. To be more animal bodies so that the virus can move from one body to another. To stay present as an animal body, to stay absent as antibody or resistance to the virus[134] invasion.

The categorical THE is also a virus mechanism, locking you in THE virus universe. EITHER/OR is another virus formula. It is always you OR the virus. EITHER/OR. This is in point of fact the conflict formula which is seen to be an archetypical virus mechanism. The proposed language will delete these virus mechanisms and make them impossible of formulation in the language. The language will be a tonal language like Chinese. It will also have a hieroglyphic script as pictorial as possible without being too cumbersome or difficult to write. This language will give one the option of silence. When not talking the user of this language can think in the silent images of the written pictorial and symbol language.

I have described here a number of weapons and tactics in the war game. Weapons that change consciousness could call the war game in question. All games are hostile. Basically there is only one game and that game is war. It's the old army game from here to eternity. Mr. Hubbard says that Scientology is a game where everybody wins. There are no games where everybody wins. That's what games are all about, winning and losing . . . The Versailles Treaty . . . Hitler dances the Occupation Jig . . . War criminals hang at Nuremberg . . . It is a rule of this game that there can be no final victory since this would mean the end of the war game. Yet every player must believe in final victory and strive for it with all his power. Faced by the nightmare of final defeat he has no alternative. So all existing technologies with escalating efficiency produce more and more total weapons until we have the atom bomb which could end the game by destroying all players. Now mock up a miracle. The so stupid players decide to save the game. They sit down around a big table and draw up a plan for the immediate deactivation and eventual destruction of all atomic weapons. Why stop there?

Conventional bombs are unnecessarily destructive if nobody else has them hein? Let's turn the war clock back to 1917:

Keep the home fires burning
Though the hearts are yearning

There's a long, long trail awinding . . .[135]

Back to the American Civil War . . .
"He has loosed the fatal lightning of his terrible swift sword."[136] His fatal lightning didn't cost as much in those days. Save a lot on the defense budget this way on back to flintlocks, matchlocks, swords, armor, lances, bows and arrows, spears, stone axes and clubs. Why stop there? Why not grow teeth and claws, poison fangs, stingers, spines, quills, beaks and suckers and stink glands and fight it out in the muck hein?

That is what this revolution is about. End of game. New games? There are no new games from here to eternity. END OF THE WAR GAME.

And now, to recapitulate: Small arms are only effective in a condition of chaos such as could be expected for example after a nuclear attack on America. The logical procedure then would be this:

Stockpile arms but do not use or go near the stockpiles until conditions occur in which small arms could be a decisive factor. Assassination by List could be highly useful if the list is accurate, since the actual orders are given by a very few people. Undoubtedly random individual assassination could be highly effective but random group assassination could provoke such countermeasures and such a reaction on the part of a terrified populace that the revolution would be in danger of total suppression.

Mass Assassination[137] I have described as a utopian fantasy based on the observation most of the trouble on this planet comes from about ten percent of the population.

If these obstructions were summarily removed we would all feel a great deal better. However in practice MA has usually been taken over by precisely the undesirable ten percent . . . so it is to be regarded as a highly dubious maneuver.

Biological and chemical weapons remain one of the most important factors, since they *can* be made in basement laboratories by anyone with the necessary training.

The weapons I wish to advocate are weapons that change consciousness—cutups, scrambling, use of videotapes, etc. The weapons of illusion.

"Nothing is true everything is permitted." Last words of Hassan-i Sabbah, the Old Man of the Mountain.


William S. Burroughs

# AFTERWORD

V. Vale

It was a huge relief—like releasing a sigh that began in 1981—to receive the news that the complete William S. Burroughs *"The Revised Boy Scout Manual": An Electronic Revolution* is being published by an academic press, fully annotated to the *n*th degree as only *professionals* can do. The reason for my intense interest is that my tiny publishing company, RE/Search, had planned to publish the full version from 1981 to 1982. Due to a personal relationship blowup and more, the project died on the vine. But not before we had enlisted the highly talented (and now deceased) Osborn brothers (Jim and Dan) to illustrate the book with handmade drawings. A few illustrations were made (I am still searching for them, hoping they can be found), but I went on to other projects. I managed to publish only the first part of *The Revised Boy Scout Manual* in my RE/Search issue #4/5. Now, having just reread the manuscript, I fervently wish RE/Search could have published it in its entirety in 1982—in all its mind-bendingly prophetic, visionary, inspiring, imaginative, and, above all, *incendiary* glory. Whew! I would think twice about being seen reading this book on an airplane, much less trying to sneak it aboard in a carry-on suitcase.

I have a theory that friends are BORN, not "made." And the quick shortcut to establishing a friendship with William S. Burroughs (who was decades older than I) was, as Goethe put it, *shared affinities*. In our case, these included hatred of authority/authoritarianism, love of solitude, and a passion for scientific knowledge of the deepest human proclivities. Therefore, we each embodied a fierce desire for independence, paranoia of one's fellow man, and, as a result, a primary passion for knowledge about self-defense and preemptive survivalist behavior—that is, see everybody before they see you! We had a mutual cosmic contempt for the status quo, antiquated language, "beliefs," economic "systems," and visual "culture" that now hold an entire planet hostage.

In our passion to learn everything possible about self-defense, we shared a love of guns and a desire to keep abreast of the state-of-the-art refinements continually being innovated by the highly competitive firearms manufacturers. Our quests for information on this subject were granular. One of the big thrills of my life was meeting Uziel Gal, inventor of the "Uzi" submachine gun, at a Bay Area Gun Show. And it was a big thrill when I was able to take a photo of William at the San Francisco Gun Exchange holding a semiautomatic (not full-auto) version of the fabled Uzi machine pistol. Both of us harbored doubts about the efficacy of the 95-grain 9mm round versus the 230-grain .45 cartridge—which was purportedly invented to "neutralize" the drug-crazed "Amoks" allegedly populating the eastern half of planet Earth. But we both agreed that the Government Model .45 automatic, carried by hundreds of thousands of U.S. soldiers during World War II and the Korean War, was almost impossible to shoot with any accuracy (although an exceptional marksman such as Mark Pauline was able to place most rounds within the bull's-eye at five yards—even usually at fifteen yards.) Then again, we knew that about 99 percent of all self-defense pistol deployment takes place under five yards, with most under a scary eight feet! And we were aware that in one second, an experienced San Quentin ex-con can cover those eight feet and take your self-defense pistol away from you—all the academic training you've obsessively endured out the window, just as all the arduous gym workouts building up cosmetically admirable musculature can instantly be nullified by an experienced street fighter who's spent half his life in and out of prison! We both knew that you never fire a pistol at an attacker once; *no,* you immediately fire two shots in the "center mass" (chest area) and a third to the head, then back up and prepare to shoot again repeatedly. Some criminals are superhuman in their strength, fortitude, and speed.

These were exact topics we discussed, and much more. Early on, William presented me with the gift of a Cobra, which is a steel handle that, with the flick of a wrist, telescopes into a sharp-tipped metal "rod" capable of breaking flesh and then some. In 1984 I took it with me on a trip to Spain, and the Spanish customs officer frowned heavily but in the end allowed me to take it in my checked luggage. William himself had flown with it; as he put it, "You need three lines of defense. I have a knife, the Cobra, and my cane." When I visited William in Lawrence, Kansas, in 1988, he showed me an illustrated hardback book titled *Cane Fighting.* He also gave me knife-throwing lessons against the shack where he stored some of his shotgun paintings. There I found a discarded spray-paint canister bearing multiple colors and asked if I could have it—and would he *autograph* it? To this day, this is one of my most cherished possessions; I store it in a drawer away from light and moisture.

It's well known that William S. Burroughs is the *éminence grise* of countercultural thinking, conceptualizing, exploring, and social experimentation, as well as an *early adopter* of *experiencing. Ayahuasca* vision-questing is enjoying a revival now, but he investigated it in the fifties and had his reports published in a 1963 City Lights chapbook titled *The Yage Letters.* Burroughs invented the term *Heavy Metal,* which is an enduring subgenre of rock 'n' roll. He coined the term *Soft Machine,* which was adopted by an avant rock band whose important members recently passed away. Surely William S. Burroughs was the first person to write the phrase "fake news," which now rules the professional media worldwide—in this very book, *The Revised Boy Scout Manual.* In 1970 he had visualized and described a whole variety of memes that could change the world's hierarchical power structures, using lowly and democratically available audio and video recorders. Currently there are almost a billion smartphones capable of making and sending meme videos and audio recordings all over the world, instantaneously.

*The Revised Boy Scout Manual* offers easy-to-read *proof* that the *uncensored* human imagination, when allowed to freely extrapolate about future social change, can offer *outrageous* scenarios and fresh language capable of inspiring readers decades into the future. Who can ever forget the crowd chanting "Bugger the Queen!" The darkest possible humor, not shying away from racial and sexual taboos, can be found within the pages of *RBSM. Contradiction,* the true foundation of our existence, is also evident: early on, William gives scenarios for ridding the earth of the 10 percent who are "shits" ruining our world. . . . Later on he reckons that those who actually *kill* these 10 percent might well end up turning into "new" versions of them. As William discovered, much to his sorrow, if you kill somebody, your life will be irrevocably changed, and your dream life will be forever haunted and transformed into the stuff of nightmares. One of the best columns of the *Police Marksman* (a slick color magazine) dealt with stories of officers who have killed criminals and then began suffering excruciating nightmares and PTSD-type traumas that begin ruining their lives and marriages and rendering them incapable of employment.

When I met William in 1981, I got the feeling that there was nobody in his life who shared his love and knowledge of firearms. So right away, I organized a trip to Chabot Gun Club in Castro Valley with a few close friends who, like me, shared what at the time was a most secret passion. The local television station KQED sent a camera team to record our little "adventure." In a short time William got to try a whole range of firearms he had read about but had never actually been able to handle and shoot. He loudly disdained the use of earplugs, and I foolishly imitated him; it took about a year for the ringing in my ears to fade away. Later on I noticed that he used large hearing-protection headsets. I brought along my recently purchased guns: a Bernardelli .25 small automatic, and the then-heavily-promoted Heckler and Koch P7. When William shot with each of them, they *both* jammed. I remember his yelling after one of the jams, "Get rid of it! Get rid of it! If a gun doesn't fire, it's worthless—it's just a club!". So right after the shoot, my friend M_____, who owned a car, took both guns to a gun store down the peninsula and sold them for cash. Nothing like learning from *experience*!

Having tracked down and read (or tried to read) almost every book that William ever recommended, I can probably with some validity describe him as a "mentor" of mine. The first time I recall seeing him give a bona fide smile was early on when I took him for breakfast to Mama's Restaurant in North Beach on the edge of Washington Square Park. At the end of the meal when we were ready to leave, I picked up the check and refused to take his money. He was genuinely *surprised,* and I got a *real* smile, not a feigned one. That smile is one of my favorite memories of the man whom I'm convinced will still be read a hundred years from now (if the world lasts that long). *Real* writers offer you a host of *ideas*—especially ideas having to do with *future freedoms*— and if your ideas are futuristic-black-humor-and-speculative-libratory, then . . .

I argue that William S. Burroughs was *the* preeminent prophet of the 20th century, and his entire opus offers testimony as to the bewildering, dazzling scope of his radical thinking and imagination, with some of the funniest dialogue that has ever been written. If you are a prophet, expect your books to be read *long* after your physical body is dead. Because, arguably, your words are YOU, and if your language lives on, in a way *you* live on. What could be better?

—V. Vale, RE/Search sole proprietor/founder,
San Francisco, November 29, 2017

# SUPPLEMENT 1

From NYPLTS 2; typescript transcribed exactly as is, including line breaks, with no corrections or edits whatsoever. Editorial notations are enclosed in square brackets.

[42]
mass media and CIA. These undercover agents stand ready for
operations of sabotage and murder. They also serve as an intelligence
net work. Most of them anonymous, unnoticed but some rise to the
top in their simulated trade or profession. Here is Danny the Cop
in his new uniform square jaw blue eyes red hair . . . He comes on his
bestial colleague kneeing a Black in the groin . . . He just looks
at them.
"Whatsa matter sonny you gotta weak stomach?"
"Hell he's new on the force. He'll find out soon enough its the
onlyway to handle these animals . . ."
I happen to believe in law enforcement and the teaching of Christ"
None of them even try to meet his gaze. He rises in the force
likea comet. He is scrupulously fair and polite at all times.
His arrest record is sensational. (We throw him heroin shipments
and frame him some Mafia wops) Our media boys give him the build
    up,

THE PERFECT AMERICAN COP . . . Chief of Police in New York
   now headed for
Governor . . .
On MA DAY he will appear on television and say . . . "Cops are
nothing but guard dogs for the rich . . . Let's all quit and go fishing
   . . ."

## [43]
And here is his brother the Priest.
When the time comes out Life Time plant will releasea spe4cial
issue denouncing the social political and economic structure of
   America
as rotten to the core . . . You see MA DAY which is known as MAD is
more than a py off for our boys. It's is above all a time of
*spirituel assassination* the shattering of alien Gods . . .
MAD is quite an occasion in America. Whole categories are
categorically eliminated: Wallace Folk, religious owmen, the
membrr of all decency and anti obscenity leagues and societyes
socit the members of all decency and anti obscenity leagues
with out exception and any bastard who givesa dime to MRA
and every species of evangelist
Wallace Folk, religious women, narcs and lawmen, the members of
all decency and anti obscenity leagues with exception and any
bastard connected with MRA, evangelists of all br and every
species of evangelist, acid throwing Mafia wops . . . And the rich
had better havea pretty clean bill of health . . . (A ord to the s wise
KICK IN NOW) and the same goes for legislators . . .

## [44]
Now MA day in America will be a thing to see. About a million in the
first wave before we can clear the air and get aour wind back then
another million just to be sure . . . I know you Black Brothers have
been looking foreward to this and you wont be disappointed . . .
Here isa little town in the deep South mid summer somnolent and
menacing thunder in the air. There is the sherriff like an old
woman man of old fibrous roots and there is his swollen with
venom like an@@@ and beside him sits his fat duputy likea vne

venomous toad swollen and heavy with it he hast kicked a Nigger
in the nuts in a month . . . They look up and there are three
Niggers in yellow silk suits standing there as if they owned the town.
on of them calls to the sherrif
"Hey boy . . . Come over here . . ."
Its too good to be true. The sheriff and his deputy move
foreward slowly hands burshing notches in their gun butts.
Then they stop when they see the machine pistols in three,
steady hands . . .
"We never done you no harm boys" says the sherriff
"I wouldnt hurt a dog unless it was biting me" says the deputy . . .

[44A]
He goes down likea sack of concrete hicupping a rope of blood . . .
A boy looks quizically down at the body of the sherriff . . .
"I think he's bleeding sap . . ."
The towns people are dumbfounded mouths open showing the yellow
tobaco stained teeth. The old fink druggist slips into the phone
booth and gets through to the sheriff's office in Cold Springs . . ,
A black boy picks up the phone and drawls . . . "This is Sherriff
Jesse Rawlings speaking . . ."
"Sherriff three mad niggers just gunned down the sherriff and his
deputy . .
"Well now I8m right sorry to hear about that were'nt two finer men in
this valley than old Clem Scranton and Luke Bane they were good old
boys but I got my hawgs to slop and after that I gotta go up to
dry gulch and help burn a Nigger and after that
I'll be seeing that little high yaller gal works in Mary Lu's
Skin Bleach and Hair Straighteing Parlor . . . Might get around to see
      you
folks next weeks some time . . ."

[45]
Norw here is an educational short . . .
THE SECOND COMING
Christ and his disciples return to the Bible Belt . . .
"They look like fairies to me . . ."

"They sure do Clem and what that filthy stuff around his head
in front of decent people?"
So they string them up one by one wrists manacled above the
head. One deputy stands in front with a blow torch and the other behi
behind reaming the ass and burning off the genitals to falsetto
obscenities and orgams noises. They save Christ for last . . .
Romeo and Juliet making love. Cops break the door down and rush in
waving guns
"And they call us animals" says the lead cop. All right boys take
the place apart . . ."
The narcs storm through the palatial room ripping pictues off the
frame breaking vases ripping tapestries to shreds . . .
"All right I found it . . ." A cop narc hold up a bottle of laudanum
"All right you two get your filthy clothes on . . ."

[46]
"WHAT ARE YOU LOOKING AT?"
A NARC
A narc kicks Romeo in his naked groin . . .
"All right take em out nekked like we find em"
Romeo is dragged out vomiting. A narc feels Juliet's tits from
behind . . .
Two beautiful boys making love . . . Narc crash through the skylight
"WHAT ARE YOU DOING IN FRONT OF DECENT PEOPLE?"
The boy looks at him his mouth open the teeth white and fragile
very thin and blue around the edges like porcelain . . .
The narc's boot crashes into his face knocking
out the front teeth . . .
"All right you filthy brown artist where is the pot stash?"
A pot sniffing fink houd tears at a boy's groin. A decency fighter
scrapes the phallus off a Greek youth on an attic vase while another
throws acid on Appallo's balls. Others step on beautiful ghurka lizards
and tear the wings off flying foxes because they look like pretty little
fairies . . . Hiroshima cuts in . . .
Now the Angels of Death ride on the Bible Belt . . . gliders,
       motorcycels,

[47]

youth of the world DEATH blazing from their eyes . . . a skeleton a
    badge
a rust gun slowly covered by leaves and dust and sand . . . DEATH,
    Johnny
come and took over . . .

[48]

They break angels wings with their clubs they tar and feather the
    young
Maize God they arrest Pan for indecent exposure . . .
When they finish the world will bea fit place for decent Wallace
folk to live in . . . Are we going to let them finish?
MAD MAD MAD DEATH TO THE UGLY AMERICAN
DEATH TO THE GRAY DIKES
DEATH TO THE EVIL OLD WOMEN

# SUPPLEMENT 2

From AZTS 1; typescript transcribed exactly as is, including line breaks, with no corrections or edits whatsoever. Editorial notations are enclosed in square brackets.

[Leaf 1]
Insert page 34  8

Speach scramblers came into use around 1882 thus antedating the first
tape recorder by seven years. Mr Hart experimented with the early
speach scramblers and designed his own models. The first model was
a simple mike inside @@ two interlocking cylinders so perforated that
the speach was cut off and emerged in accordance with the perferation
patterns. When he heard the first tape recorder in 1899 it all clicked
into place: a way to be THE VOICE inside the head of every human
    dog
on this planet. The first tape recorder was described as impractical
and Hart saw that it stayed that way. In secret laboratories he put
his techicians to work perfecting the machine so when the tape
recorder hit the open ~~maret££~~ market in the 1940s after World War
    Two
he was years ahead with his private research. And his research had

shown him the way to control the use of this machine and discourage
any experiments with speech scrambling and tape recorder cut ups.
He monoplized new discoveries in this way to give himself a
    comfortable

[Leaf 2]
Insert page 34   13

perferential point of attack: an electronic revolution. Soon mass
produced @@ video cameras and projectros will be within the reach of
millions of people. They can start making their own show and their
    own
reality. Take you video camera into the streets around you. Now
cut into those streets any scenes you want. Take your video tape and
camera back into the streets and take the reaction to that. This could
lead to street theatre on a mass scale drawing in the mass media.

# SUPPLEMENT 3

From NYPLTS 2; typescript transcribed exactly as is, including line breaks, with no corrections or edits whatsoever. Editorial notations are enclosed in square brackets.

[51]
. . .
"I CAN <u>BREATHE"</u>
And the SS elite guard travelled in time as well intercepting
the shits before they could get a foothoold.
Here is a team of 16 trained guerilla fighters. Since they
will be isolted together for years at a time they are all
homosexual paired off aacording to precise reciprocity of
sexual preferences after exhaustive but not unpleasnat tests
at the Sexual Institute. (This ervise of finding suitable
mates for every man is available to all) . . . Camera pans over
the intent youg faces . . . An educational short to show the
nature of the enemy . . .
A shy beatiful Indian boy with an inocent smile hold out a basket
of fruit to bearded Conquistadores. Brutal soldiers shoves
him down onto stump and cut both his hands off . . . Plenty
more like that. Its the final briefing now . . .

[51]

notches . . . religious women . . . decency leagues . . . antiobscenity
    drives . . .
You poison the air we breathe . . . Wipe out the Bible Belt and you
    will
glimpse the Garden of Eden . . .
"It was like being cured of clap after twenty dripping years" said
a dazed bystander . . . Happy smiling faces @@@@ from sea to
    shinning
sea . . . [the 4 "@" symbols strike out the word "all"]
And now back to merrie England and getting merrier by the minute
as the Shit Slaughter Guard goes to work . . .
Office of the SS Demolition Unit . . .
"Investigation has convinced us that the so called Neurological
and Encephallographic Institute in emmitting shit brain waves on
a massive basis . . . Old duffer there has'nt utr turned up anything
useful in twenty years . . . No work with autonomic shapping . . .
We urge an immediate therapeutic test . . ."
"Its expensive equipment. Couldnt we simply take it over and use it?"
"It would take our best computer men weeks to trace down and
    deactivate
or replace the shit programming . . . Any attempt before that time
to use the installation for the broadcast of anti shot would

[52]

Use the installation for wholesome purposes would activate whole
batteries of @@@@ . .:: . . . interconnected shit programs . . . Proceed
at once with the only remedy . . . Demolish the shit installation . . ."
Cars draw up in front of the Institute . . .
"Who did you wish to speak to?"
The SS guard does not answer her directly. He speaks into a
mike . . .
"Notice to all personell on these premesis . . . You have ten minutes
to vacate . . . You may carry nothing with you but your clothes . . .
No books papers or notes of any kind . . . You will be searched at
the door . . . Notice to all personelll . . . You have ten minutes to
vacate . . ."

And now the Professor himself rushes out of his study . . .
"But what is the meaning of this? We are a scientific institute . . ."
The SS guard repeats into his mike . . . "Notice to all personell . . .
You have ten minutes to vacate these £££££ premesis . . ."
The presonell are loaded into cars, charges placed and the institute
goes up in chunks . . .

@@@@@@@@@@@@@@@@@@@@@@@@@@@@ to a rousing
rendition of altered reality . . . Old men dance naked in the streets

[53]
"YIPPEE . . . THIS IS THE FIRST HARD ON I'VE HAD IN
    TWENTY YEARS . . ."

# SUPPLEMENT 4

From AZTS 1; photocopied typescript transcribed exactly as is with no corrections or edits whatsoever—with the sole exception of the line endings. Editorial notations are enclosed in square brackets.

. . . . Now to make this scanning process conscious and controllable, try this:

Walk down a city block with a camera and take what you notice, moving the camera around as closely as possible to follow the direction of your eye. The point is to make the camera your eyes and take what your eyes are scanning out of the larger picture. At the same time take the street at wide angle from a series of still positions. The street of the operator is, of course, the street as seen by the operator. It is, of course, differend from the street seen at wide angle. Much of it is in fact missing. Now you can make arbitrary scanning patterns—that is cover first one side of the street and then the other in accordance with a preconceived plan. So you are breaking down the automatic scanning patters. You could also make colour scanning patterns, that is, scan out green, blue, red, etc. in so far as you can with your camera. That is, you are using an arbitrary pre-conceived scanning pattern, in order to break down automatic scanning patterns. A number of operators do this and then scramble in their takes together and with wide angle tapes. This could train the subject to see at a wider angle and also to ignore and erase at will. ¶ [holographic paragraph symbol]

Now all this is readily subject to experimental verification on control subjects. Nor need the equipment be all that complicated. I have shown how it could work with feedback from brainwaves and visceral response and video tape photos of subject taken while he is seeing and hearing the tape, simply to show optimum effectiveness. You can start with two tape recorders. The simplest scrambling device is sissors and splicing equipment. You can start scrambling words, make any kind of tapes and scramble them and observe the effects on friends and on yourself. Next step is sound film and then video camera. Of course results from individual experiments could lead to mass experiments, mass fear tapes, riot tapes, etc. The possibilities here for research and experiment are virtually unlimited and I have simply made a few very simple suggestions. ¶ [holographic paragraph symbol]

A virus is characterised and limited by obligate cellular parasitism. All viruses must parasitize living cells for their replication. For all viruses the infection cycle comprises entry into the host, intracellular replication, and escape from the body of the host to initiate a new cycle in a fresh host. I am quoting here from <u>Mechanisms of Virus Infection</u> edited by Dr. Wilson Smith. In its wild state the virus has not proved to be a very adaptable organism. Some viruses have burned themselves out since they were 100 per cent fatal and there were no resevoirs. Each strain of virus is rigidly programmed for a certain attack on certain tissues. If the attack fails, the virus does not gain a new host. There are of course virus mutations, and the influenza virus has proved quite versatile in this way. Generally it's the simply repetition of the same method of entry, and if that method is blocked by any body or other agency such as interferon, the attack fails. By and large, our virus is a stupid organism. Now we can think for the virus, devise a number of alternate methods of entry. For example, the host is simultaneously attacked by an ally virus who tells him that everything is alright and by a pain and fear virus. So the virus is now using an old method of [there follow here approximately nine words that are almost completely cut off in the photocopy and are illegible]

We have considered the possibility that a virus is can be activated or even created by [the phrase "can. . . . by" is holographic insert] very small units of sound and image. So conceived, the virus can be made to order in the laboratory. Ah, but for the takes to be effective, you must have also the actual virus and what is this so actual virus. New viruses turn up from time to time but from ["from" is holographic insert] where do they turn up? Well, let's see how we could make a virus turn up. We plot now our virus's symptoms and make a scramble tape. The most susceptible, that is those who reproduce some of the desired symptoms, will then be scrambled into more tapes till we scramble our virus into existence. This birth of a virus occurs when our virus is able to reproduce itself in a host and pass itself on to another host. Perhaps too, with the virus under laboratory control it can be tamed for useful purposes. Imagine for example, a sex virus. It so inflames the sex centres in the back brain that the host is driven mad from sexuality, all other considerations are blacked out. Parks full of naked, frenzied people, shitting, pissing, ejaculating, and screaming. So the virus could be malignant, blacking out all regulations and end in exhaustion, convulsions, and death.

Now let us attempt the same thing with tape. We organize a sex-tape festival. 100,000 people bring their scrambled sex tapes, and video tapes as well, to scramble in together. Projected on vast screens, muttering out over the crowd, sometimes it slows down so you see a few seconds, then scrambled again, then slow down, scramble. Soon it will scramble them all naked. The cops and the National Guard are stripping down. LETS GET OURSELVES SOME CIVIES. Now a thing like that could be messy, but those who survive it recover from the madness. Or, say a small select group of really like-minded people get together with their sex tapes, you see the process is now being brought under control. And the fact that anybody can do it is in itself a limiting factor.

Here is Mr. Hart, who wants to infect everyone with his own image and turn them all into himself, so he scrambles himself and dumps himself out in search of worthy vessels. If nobody else knows about scrambling techniques he might scramble himself quite a stable of replicas. [ts has "seplicas" with holographic "r" over ts "s"] But anybody can do it. So go on, scramble your sex words out, and find suitable mates.

If you want to, scramble yourself out there, every stale joke, fart, chew, sneeze, and stomach rumble. If your trick no work you better run. Everybody doing it, they all scramble in together and the populations of the earth just settles down to a nice even brown colour. Scrambles is the democratic way, the way of full cellular representation. Scrambles is the American way. ¶ INSERT ¶ [the two ¶ marks and "INSERT" are holographic inserts]

Ron Hubbard, founder of scientology, says that certain wrods and word combinations can produce serious illnesses and mental disturbances. I can claim some skill in the scrivener's trade, but I cannot guarentee to write a passage that will make someone physically ill. If Mr. Hubbard's claim is justified, this is certainly a matter for further research, and we can easily find out experimentally whether his claim is justified or not. Mr. Hubbard bases the power he attributes to words on his theory of engrams. An engram is defined as word, ["word" is holographic correction of ts "work"] sound, image recorded by the subject in a period of pain and unconsciousness. Some of this material may be reassuring: I think he's going to be alright. Reassuring material is an ally engram, and ["and" is holographic correction of ts "and al"] ally engrams, ["s" is holographic addition to ts "engram"] according to Mr. Hubbard, are ["are" is holographic correction of ts "is"] just as abberative ["abberative" is holographic correction of ts "effective"] as [a] [the word "a" struck out here] hostile pain engrams. ["s" is holographic addition to ts "engram"] Any part of this recording played back to the subject later will reactivate operation pain, he may actually develop a headache and feel depressed, anxious, or tense. Well, Mr. Hubbard's engram theory is very easily subject to experimental verification. Take ten volunteer subjects, subject them to a pain stimulus accompanied by certain words and sounds and images. You can in face act out little skits.

¶ [¶ symbol is holographic insert, as are quotation marks in following four sentences] "Quickly nurse, before I lose my little nigger," bellows the southern surgeon, and now a beefy white hand falls on the fragile black shoulder. "Yes, he's going to be alright. He's going to pull through."

¶ [¶ symbol is holographic insert] "If I had my way I'd let these animals die on the operating table."

¶ [¶ symbol is holographic insert] "You do not have your way, you have to do your duty as a doctor, we must do everything in our power to same human lives." And so forth.

Its the tough cop and the con cop. The ally engram is ineffective without the pain engram, just as the con cop's arm around your shoulder, his soft persuasive voice in your ear, are indeed sweet nothings without the tough cop's blackjack. Now to what extent can words recorded during medical unconsciousness be recalled during hypnosis or scientological processing? To what extent does the playback of this material effect the subject unpleasantly? Is the effect enhanced by scrambling the material, pain and ally, at very short intervals? It would seem that a scrambled engrams picture could almost dump an operating scene right in the subject's lap. Mr. Hubbard has charted his version of what he calls the reactive mind. This is roughly similar to Freud's id, a sort of built-in self defeating mechanism. As set forth by Mr Hubbard this consists of a number of quite ordinary phrases. He claims that reading these phrases, or hearing them spoken, can cause illness, and gives this as his reason for not publishing this material. Is he perhaps saying that these are magic words? Spells, in fact? If so they could be quite a weapon scrambled up with imaginative sound-and-image track. Here now is the magic that turns men into swine. To be an animal: a lone pig grunts, shits, squeals and slobbers down garbage. To be animals: a chorus of a thousand pigs. Cut that in with video tape police pictures and play it back to them and see if you get a reaction from this so reactive mind.

Now here is another. To be a body, well its sure an attractive body, rope the marks in. And a nice body symphony to go with it, rhythmic heart beats, contented stomach rumbles. To be bodies: recordings and pictures of hideous, aged, diseased bodies farting, pissing, shitting, groaning, dying. To do everything: man in a filthy apartment surrounded by unpaid bills, unanswered letters, jumps up and starts washing dishes and writing letters. To do nothing: he slumps in a chair, jumps up, slumps in chair, jumps up. Finally slumps in a chair, drooling in idiot helplessness, while he looks at the disorder piled around him. The reactive mind commands can also be used to advantage with illness tapes. While projecting past coldsore onto the subject's face, and playing back to him a past illness tape, you can say: to be me, to be you, to stay here, to stay there, to be a body, to be bodies, to stay in, to stay out, to stay present, to stay absent. To what extent are these reactive mind phrases when scrambled effective in causing disagreeable symptoms in control volunteer subjects? As to Mr. Hubbard's claims for the reactive mind, only research can give us the answers.

# SUPPLEMENT 5

Extracts from William S. Burroughs, *Electronic Revolution,* 10th ed. (Bonn: Expanded Media Editions, 1998) transcribed exactly as is with no corrections or edits whatsoever. Editorial notations are enclosed in square brackets.

. . .

In the *Electronic Revolution* I advance the theory that a virus is a very small unit of word and image. I have suggested now such units can be biologically activated to act as communicable virus strains. Let us start with three tape recorders in The Garden of Eden. Tape recorder 1 is Adam. Tape recorder 2 is Eve. Tape recorder 3 is God, who deteriorated after Hiroshima into the Ugly American. Or to return to our primeval scene: Tape recorder 1 is the male ape in a helpless sexual frenzy as the virus strangles him. Tape recorder 2 is the cooing female ape who straddles him. Tape recorder 3 is DEATH.

Steinplatz postulates that the virus of biologic mutation, which he calls Virus B-23, is contained in the word. Unloosing this virus from the word could be more deadly that unloosing the power of the atom. Because all hate all pain all fear all lust is contained in the word. Perhaps we have here in these three tape recorders the virus of biologic mutation which once gave us the word and has hidden behind the word ever since. And perhaps three tape recorders and some good biochemists can unloose this force. Now look at these three tape recorders and think in terms of the virus particle. Recorder 1 is the perspective host for an influenza virus. Tape recorder number 2 is the means by which the virus gains access to the host, in the case of a flu virus by dissolving a hole in cells of the host's respiratory tract. Number 2, having gained access to the cell, leads in number 3. Number 3 is the effect produced in the host by the virus: coughing, fever, inflammation. *Number 3 is objective reality produced by the virus in the host.* Viruses make themselves real. It's a way viruses have. We now have three tape recorders. So we will make a simple word virus. Let us suppose that our target is a rival politician. On tape recorder 1 we will record speeches and conversation carefully editing in stammers mispronouncing, inept phrases . . . the worst number 1 can assemble. Now on tape recorder 2 we will make so a love tape by bugging his bed room. We can potentiate this tape by splicing it in with a sexual object that is inadmissible or inaccessible or both, say the senator's teenage daughter. On tape recorder 3 we will record hateful disapproving voices and splice the three recordings in together at very short intervals and play them back to the senator and his constituents. This cutting and playback can be very complex involving speech scramblers and batteries of tape recorders *but the basic principle is simply splicing sex tape and disapproval tapes in together.* Once the association lines are established they are activated every time the senator's speech centres are activated which is all the time heaven help that sorry bastard if anything happened to his big mouth. So his teenage daughter crawls all over him while Texas rangers and decent church-going women rise from tape recorder 3 screaming "WHAT ARE YOU DOING IN FRONT OF DECENT PEOPLE."

The teen age daughter is just a refinement. Basically all you need is sex recordings on number 2 and hostile recordings on number 3. With this simple formula any CIA sonofabitch can become God that is tape recorder 3. Notice the emphasis on sexual material in burglaries and bugging in the Watergate cess pool . . . Bugging Martin Luther King's bedroom . . . Kiss kiss bang bang . . . A deadly assassination technique. At the very least sure to unnerve and put opponents at a disadvantage.

. . .

I have made a number of experiments with street recordings and playback over a period of years and the startling fact emerges *that you do not need sex recordings or even doctored tapes to produce effects by playback. Any recordings played back on location in the manner I will now describe can produce effects.* No doubt sexual and doctored tapes would be more powerful. But some of the power in the word is released by simple playback as anyone can verify who will take the time to experiment . . . I quote from some notes on these playback experiments.

Friday July 28, 1972 . . . Plan 28 at a glance . . . First some remarks on the tape recorder experiments started by Ian Sommerville in 1965. These involved not only street, pub, party, subway recordings but also *playback* on location. When I returned to London from the States in 1966 he had already accumulated a considerable body of data and developed a technology. He had discovered that playback on location can produce definite effects.

Playing back recordings of an accident can produce another accident. In 1966 I was staying at the Rushmore Hotel, 11 Trebovir Road, Earl's Court, and we carried out a number of these operations: street recordings, cut in of other material, playback in the streets . . . (I recall I had cut in fire engines and while playing this tape back in the street fire engines passed.) These experiments were summarized in THE INVISIBLE GENERATION . . . (I wonder if anybody but CIA agents read this article or thought of putting these techniques into actual operation.) Anybody who carries out similar experiments over a period of time will turn up more "coincidences" than the law of averages allows. The tech can be extended by taking still or moving pictures as the recordings are made and more pictures during playback. I have frequently observed that this simple operation—make recordings and take pictures of some location you wish to discommode or destroy, now play recordings back and take more pictures —, will result in accidents, fires, removals. Especially the latter. The target moves. We carried out this operation with the Scientology Center at 37 Fitzroy Street. Some months later they moved to 68 Tottenham Court Road, where a similar operation was recently carried out . . .

Here is a sample operation carried out against The Moka Bar at 29 Frith Street London W1 beginning on August 3, 1972 . . . Reverse Thursday . . . Reason for operation was outrageous and unprovoked discourtesy and poisoned cheese cake . . .

Now to close in on The Moka Bar. Record. Take pictures. Stand around outside. Let them see me. They are seething around in there. The horrible old proprietor, his frizzy-haired wife and slack-jawed son, the snarling counter man. I have them and they know it.

"You boys have a rep for making trouble. Well come on out and make some. Pull a camera breaking act and I'll call a Bobby. I gotta right to do what I like in the public street."

If it came to that I would explain to the policeman that I was taking street recordings and making a documentary of Soho. This was after all London's First Expresso Bar was it not? I was doing them a favor. They couldn't say what both of us knew without being ridiculous . . .

"He's not making any documentary. He's trying to blow up the coffee machine, start a fire in the kitchen, start fights in here, get us a citation from the Board of Health."

Yes I had them and they knew it. I looked in at the old Prop and smiled as if he would like what I was doing. Playback would come later with more pictures. I took my time and strolled over to the Brewer Street Market where I recorded a three card Monte Game. Now you see it now you don't.

Playback was carried out a number of times with more pictures. Their business fell off. They kept shorter and shorter hours. October 30, 1972 The Moka Bar closed. The location was taken over by The Queens Snack Bar.

Now to apply the 3 tape recorder analogy to this simple operation. Tape recorder 1 is the Moka Bar itself in its pristine condition. Tape recorder 2 is *my recordings* of the Moka Bar vicinity. These recordings are *access*. Tape recorder 2 in the Garden of Eden was Eve made from Adam. So a recording made from the Moka Bar is a piece of the Moka Bar. The recording once made, this piece becomes autonomous and out of their control. Tape recorder 3 is *playback*. Adam experiences shame when his *disgraceful behavior is played back to him* by tape recorder 3 which is God. By playing back my recordings to the Moka Bar when I want and with any changes I wish to make in the recordings, I become God for this local. I effect them. They cannot effect me. And what part do photos take in this operation? Recall what I said earlier about the written and spoken word. *The written word is an image is a picture*. The spoken word could be defined as any verbal units that correspond to these pictures and could in fact be extended to *any sound units that correspond* to the pictures . . . Recordings and pictures are tape recorder 2 which is access. Tape recorder 3 is playback and "reality." For example suppose your bathroom and bedroom are bugged and rigged with hidden infrared cameras. These pictures and recordings give access. You may not experience shame during defecation and intercourse but you may well experience shame when these recordings are played back to a disapproving audience.

Now let us consider the arena of politics and the applications of bugging in this area. Of course any number of recordings are immediately available since politicians make speeches on TV. However, these recordings do not give access. The man who is making a speech is not really there. Consequently more intimate or at least private recordings are needed which is why the Watergate conspirators had to resort to burglary. A presidential candidate is not a sitting duck like a Moka Bar. He can make any number of recordings of his opponents. So the game is complex and competitive with recordings made by both sides. This leads to more sophisticated techniques the details of which have yet to come out.

The basic operation of recording pictures, more pictures and playback can be carried out by anyone with a recorder and a camera. Any number can play. Millions of people carry out this basic operation could nullify the control system which those who are behind Watergate and Nixon are attempting to impose. Like all control systems it depends on maintaining a monopoly position. If anybody can be tape recorder 3 then tape recorder 3 loses power. God must be *The* God.

# ABBREVIATIONS AND SOURCES

NYPLTS 1—*The Revised Boy Scout Manual,* ts in WSB typing with WSB holographic edits, thirty-six leaves, in the Berg Collection at the New York Public Library.

NYPLTS 2—*The Revised Boy Scout Manual,* ts in WSB typing, approximately sixty-two leaves, in the Berg Collection at the New York Public Library. This is clearly an earlier draft of materials refined in NYPLTS 1.

AZTS 1—*The Revised Boy Scout Manual,* pc ts of NYPLTS 1, approximately fifty leaves, but with differing edits also in WSB's hand, with several pages not found in NYPLTS 1, in the Archives and Special Collections Library at Arizona State University Library. It includes two appended leaves, transcribed in Supplement 2.

AZTS 2—Pc ts of materials related to NYPLTS 1 and AZTS 1, approximately sixty-seven leaves, in the Archives and Special Collections Library at Arizona State University Library. This is clearly a very early group of sketches, some of which were further developed on NYPLTS 1 and AZTS 1.

Vale—Printouts in the style of galleys for *The Revised Boy Scout Manual,* which were intended to form a book-length edition of *RBSM.* Typesetting by Vale. A short selection from the beginning of this version was published in Vale's serial, *RE/SEARCH* 4/5 (1982), republished 2007.

Three 90-minute cassette tapes, "WSBURROUGHS: THE REVISED BOY SCOUT MANUAL," "copied by Vale from cassettes supplied by Genesis P-Orridge," in the Rare Books and MSS Library, The Ohio State University Libraries, in which WSB reads large portions of *The Revised Boy Scout Manual,* at times including references to punctuation, upper case, and so forth.

Burroughs, William S., *Electronic Revolution* [Sl]: Collection Ohio University, 1971. "Published for Henri Chopin." Source for the passages is inserted in *RBSM.*

Burroughs, William S., *Electronic Revolution,* (Bonn: Expanded Media Editions, 1998). Source of the introduction is excerpted in Supplement 5. Numerous editions published starting in 1970.

SB—Smith & Bennett; refers to this edition.

# NOTES

## NOTES TO THE FOREWORD

1. William S. Burroughs et Daniel Odier, *Entretiens: Avec William Burroughs* (Paris: Éditions Pierre Belfond, 1969), 11.

2. William S. Burroughs, *Interzone* (London: Penguin, 1989), 17.

3. Robin Lyndenberg, *Word Cultures: Radical Theory and Practice in William S. Burroughs' Fiction* (Urbana: University of Illinois Press, 1987), 45.

4. Sabine Müller, "Body Integrity Identity Disorder (BIID)—Is the Amputation of Healthy Limbs Ethically Justified?" *American Journal of Bioethics* 9.1 (2009): 36–43.

5. Frédérique de Vignemont, "Bodily Awareness," *The Stanford Encyclopedia of Philosophy* (Fall 2011 Edition), ed. Edward N. Zalta. Forthcoming. http://plato.stanford.edu/archives/fall2011/entries/bodily-awareness/.

6. From now on, *RBSM* stands for *The Revised Boy Scout Manual*.

7. Dave Teeuwen, "The Soft Machines." *RealityStudio, A William S. Burroughs Community*. http://realitystudio.org/criticism/the-soft-machines/ (accessed September 17, 2011), n.p.

8. Barry Miles, *El Hombre Invisible* (London: Virgin, 1993), 192. For more references about the models for *The Wild Boys*, see "Maggs Rare Books," *Printed Catalogues, Book Catalogues*. http://www.maggs.com/catalogues/ (accessed September 17, 2011), n.p.

9. In this respect, Jamie Russel states on page 240 of his PhD thesis, "Bodies of Light: Homosexuality, Masculinity and Ascesis in the Novels of William S. Burroughs" (University of London, 2000):

"The transition from rigidity to fluidity is the key concern of The Western Lands; the bodies of the Wild Boys and Johnsons—which have always been on the verge of becoming hypermasculine, rigid and hard like the clone—are finally replaced by transcendent bodies of 'light' that are immune to the dangerous, viral influences of the feminine and to the regulation imposed by power. The body of light is transfigured in both its escape from the Law and in its immutable nature. Lacking materiality, it can no longer be conditioned, drugged or regulated by the heterosexual dominant."

10. Georges Didi-Huberman, "The Paradox of the Phasmid." *Tympanum* 3 (1999). http://www.usc.edu/dept/comp-lit/tympanum/3/phasmid.html (accessed September 17, 2011), n.p.

11. Richard Blum, *"The House by The Water." The Fourth Ghost Book,* ed. James Turner (London: Pan, 1968).

## NOTES TO "THE REVISED BOY SCOUT MANUAL"

1. NYPTS 1 has the following annotation following title: "Cover shows a boy scout with a bowie knife at his belt burning the American flag, the Union Jack, the hammer and sickle in a fire of dead leaves."

2. Old S. A. song: refers to the *Sturmabteilung* (SA), or "Brown Shirts," the original Nazi paramilitary organization.

3. Hassan I Sabbah: Hassan-i Sabbah, 1050s–1124, Persian missionary, founded group called *Hashshashin.*

4. Maurice Gustave Gamelin, 1872–1958, Commander-in-Chief of the French armed forces during World War II.

5. The Easter 1916 uprising for Irish independence, led by the Irish Republican Brotherhood, which led to the formation of the Irish Republican Army (IRA).

6. 1948 in NYPLTS 1 changed to 1848. Refers to international liberal and revolutionary movements of 1848.

7. Ernesto "Che" Guevara, 1928–67, Argentine revolutionary, an important figure in the Cuban Revolution; Giuseppe Garibaldi, 1807–82, leader of the unification of Italy; Simón Bolívar, 1783–1830, leader of the independence wars throughout South America.

8. Emended from "Canade à l'orànge."

9. Brion Gysin, 1916–86, avant-garde artist and writer, who, with WSB, refined and promoted the cutup technique used in textual and media experiments. He was a long-time friend and colleague of Burroughs.

10. Emended from "parana."

11. Naga virus: several viruses are associated with this name (including a computer virus); it is often called the "Egyptian streak virus."

12. Erwin Johannes Eugen Rommel, 1891–1944, a German field marshal during World War II and head of the Afrika Korps.

13. WSB typescript reads "to starve," later changed in NYPLTS 1 by WSB to "to stop."

14. *The Job: Interviews with William S. Burroughs,* a book of interviews with WSB by Daniel Odier (Grove Press, 1970); first published in France, 1969. In the 1974 expanded Grove Press edition, there are several pages, starting with page 62, describing experiments with infrasound and its potential use as a weapon.

15. Vladimir Gavreau, a French scientist who worked on infrasound and its biological effects in the 1960s.

16. The word "organic" inserted by WSB in NYPLTS 1 but not read on tape.

17. Wilhelm Reich, 1897–1957, controversial Austrian psychoanalyst, who developed the Orgone Box as a way to harness cosmic energy.

18. "[1.]" added by editors.

19. Rules and Simpson's: a high-end London restaurant.

20. Horn and Hardart: a New York- and Philadelphia-based restaurant, the first automat restaurant.

21. Kris: an Indonesian dagger.

22. SS: apparently refers to the Waffen SS, armed wing of the Nazi Party.

23. The number "[3.]" added by editors. From NYPLTS 2.

24. On tape recording, WSB says "occurring."

25. It is not clear exactly which doctors WSB is referring to here. "Engel" might be B. T. Engel; "Kamika" is likely Atsunori Kamiya; there are several O'Neills doing autonomic research; there are several doctors, named both Laing and Lang, doing autonomic shaping or related research; and there is a Burden Neurological Foundation in Bristol, England, which had a W. Grey Walter on its staff.

26. Royal Crowns and Royal Cavaliers: there have been several gangs in the United States and England with these or very similar names.

27. Claridge's is a luxury hotel in Mayfair, London. WSB does not use an apostrophe.

28. White's is a London Gentlemen's club.

29. There is a long line of Lord Stanfields.

30. Possibly a reference to the long line of English Charringtons.

31. *Lebensraum*: "living space"; concept used by the Nazi regime to justify territorial expansion.

32. NYPLTS 2 has "sit there," and NYPLTS 1 has "sit, their" with holographic change to "sit, there." Comma after "there" added by editors.

33. Legible, tape-recorded, or from the AZTS 1, parts of crossed-out passage follow here. "Tristam Zara" should be Tristan Tzara, 1896–1963, Romanian and French avant-garde and Dadaist poet and artist. The passage reads: . . . to be ~~taken personally by the English and result in expulsion as not in the public interest. But I think there~~

is a residue of fair minded people in England who read it as it is
intended as an empirical, sociological observation. If an image or
symbol is widely venerated in a population segment the desecration
and shattering of that image or symbol will shatter the social structure in so far as that structure is based on the image or symbol. It's
a very old rule: shatter the idols and you move in this game; shatter
the idols and you shatter the social structure. The idols are not often
as easy to find. "Bugger Nixon" just doesn't do it at all. No shock
value there.

[*WSB tape*: The cut-ups date to [*or*] and] the Dadaist movement,
and Tristram Zara pulling a poem out of a hat. So you will see this
is actually a repetition of [*WSB tape*: "Burn the Louvre"] [*"Burn
the Louvre" is a slogan originating in the Dadaist movement and
associated with Tristan Tzara; it is still used today in radical art circles.*] and everybody says, so who cares, you don't have a basically
important symbol. The tactic must shock and enrage, preferably to
the point of madness. That is what this tactic is about, desecration
madness.

34. Publius Cornelius Tacitus, ca. 56–117, Roman senator and historian.

35. See Supplement 1, pages 52–55, from NYPLTS 2, pages 42–48;
undeveloped draft texts re MA and related topics.

36. John Birch: refers to The John Birch Society, an American ultracon-
servative political advocacy group founded by Robert W. Welch, Jr.
It was especially active in the 1960s.

37. WSB changed "stinking" to "finking" in NYPLTS 1.

38. WSB changed "wogs" to "wops" in NYPLTS 1.

39. MRA: a conservative "men's rights" movement, with beginnings in
the early 20th century. The initials stand for "Men's Rights Activ-
ism." At the time WSB was writing, it was largely focused on com-
bating the rise of feminism.

40. Boer: Afrikaans word for *farmer,* designating Dutch-speaking resi-
dents of South Africa.

41. Aftosa: foot-and-mouth disease, a highly contagious viral disease of
cattle and almost all other cloven-footed domestic animals.

42. There are three pages here in NYPLTS 2 NOT in SB version; pages
51, 51 [*sic*], 52, transcribed as Supplement 3; note the redundant
page number—should be 51, 52, 53. The passage from ". . . said a
dazed bystander." to "Cut off his power." is not in NYPLTS 2.

43. Jeremy Bentham, 1748–1832, British philosopher, jurist, and social
reformer. Today, the body is on display at UCL fully clothed, but the
head is locked away securely. A wax replica head is used on the body.

44. NYPLTS 1 has "duckblow," corrected holographically by WSB to
read "duckload."

45. "And . . . hole." is NYPLTS 1 insert on a separate page in NYPLTS
1. A "marl hole" is a pit from which clay has been extracted.

46. In the passage from "In all walks of life . . ." to ". . . the penis are precisely charted," NYPLTS 2 has a number of additional phrases; that entire passage from NYPLTS 2 follows here (original errors have been retained in this passage):

In all walks of life the SS Personell Units do their work . . . in the stately homes and the best clubs . . . in kiosks, shops, pubs and coffee bars . . . A witch hunt? Exactly . . . Four or five evil old biddies can bring downa a whole quarter of London . . . the SS does its work and goes. They leave behind them happy smiling faces and hearts at peace under an English heaven they died and left to you this heath this calm this quiet scene the memory of what has been and never more will be . . . Soon even the memory of those shits will fade into air into thin air . . . The fileds of England are heavy and rich with their bone ½ meal and our happy hogs are fat and firm with theri flesh . . .

Now to put our program in operation. The food in England is now fit only for the consumption of an underpriviledged @@@@ [3-letter word struck out under 4 @ signs] vulture . . . We @@@@@@@@@@@@@@ [words struck out under 15 @ signs] will give people good food . . . Of course our world famous shit fed hogs are a first step in that direction. Ther Their flesh is rich and succulent belching up those shits afterwards makes you feel good all over . . . Long Pig we call it. It stays with you for hours . . . If there is one thing England has its plenty of water. So build fish ponds everywhere and stock them with bass 2/3 and jack salmon and perch. England becomes an anglers paradise. Close down some factories too we wont need them with the turist business we'll soon be doing.

We will give people a place to live. Weeding out five million shits givea few take a few is a long step in that £ direction. @@@@@@@@@@@@@@ [words struck out under 14 @ signs] All out birth control. Level off the populatio at 20,000,000.

We will give people SEX. The first step is to bring people with reciprocal tastes and or objectives together. When they try to do his now through ads in the underground some olf shit from Svotland yard will put them in jail. Well those shits of course were taken care of the first glad rush of MA. We set up computerized guidance centers. We set up community centers for the @@@@@@@@ [words struck out under 8 @ signs] exchange of home sex movies. What ever your thing is we will find some one to do it with you.

At the Sexual Institute we teach people how to enjoy sex. Here is a 16 year olf boy naked in a chair. Brain waves, heart rate, blood pressure recorded electrode attached to the penis. Now we show him sex pictures and those that geta reaction are repated elaborated zeroed in until the boy ejaculates.

47. L. Ron Hubbard, 1911–86, science fiction author and controversial founder of the Church of Scientology. He created a self-help system called Dianetics.

48. Brion Gysin (1916–86), *The Process* (New York: Doubleday, 1969). A novel.

49. DE: Do Easy, a discipline described by WSB in various places and featured in a short film by Gus Van Sant, *The Discipline of D.E.*

50. Carlos Castaneda, *The Teachings of Don Juan: A Yaqui Way of Knowledge* (University of California Press, 1968). WSB TS: WSB had written the title as *A Yackie Way of Knowing* but then struck it out and corrected it; he also spelled the author's name as "Castenado."

51. Two "1s" appear here and below. In general, the numbering throughout is inconsistent.

52. End of NYPLTS 2. There are several minor differences in phraseology throughout the preceding few pages. Passages that follow here which refer to NYPLTS 2 are found earlier in that TS.

53. NYPLTS 2 has, typed, "Genua." On the tape WSB pronounces this as "ghenau" [nawa]. NYPLTS 1 has a rather illegible holographic insert here, which appears to be Genau, Genvan, Genuan, or Ghanan. It would appear to be a reference to the Gnaoua or Gnawa musicians from Morocco's Atlas Mountains, who were much admired by WSB and his friends in Tangiers and who have since become well known internationally through their many recordings.

54. Refers to U.S. government drug-treatment center in Lexington, Kentucky, opened in 1935. Called The Narcotic Farm, it was closed in the 1970s.

55. Chiang Kai-shek, 1887–1975, Chairman of the National Government of China, based in Taiwan. NYPL TS 2 has the name as "Chiang Kai Check."

56. NYPLTS 2 has "hid."

57. WSB has written "INSERT" here in NYPLTS 1. Nothing is inserted here, except for the reference to "*The Unspeakable Mr. Hart.*" This is the original title of material published as a comic strip or graphic novel, illustrated by Malcolm McNeill, parts of which appeared in comic strip form in the 1970s in the British magazine *Cyclops*. It was later published in text form only in WSB's *Ah Pook Is Here and Other Texts* (London: John Calder and Riverrun Press, 1979). In 2010, Fantagraphics Books published the original comic strips under the original title of *The Unspeakable Mr. Hart.* In *Ah Pook Is Here,* there is the following passage: "The Red Fever attacks the rage centers, producing in susceptible subjects fulminating apoplexy and massive internal hemorrhaging. At an American First rally, Reddies in Boy Scout uniforms leap onto the podium. / 'A scout is clean, brave and reverent.'/ They shit on the podium and wipe their asses with Old Glory. The delegates are speechless. Their faces get redder and redder. Blood vessels rupture, eyes pop out. Hot blood spurting

from mouth and anus, they fall in steaming piles like boiled lobsters." Cf. Supplements 1 and 2 for further material not included in WSB's later versions of this passage.

58. DOR: Deadly Orgone Radiation; cf. note 17 above re Reich's Orgone Box.

59. Alamut: a fort or castle in a region in Iran, controlled for many years by Hassan-i Sabbah.

60. A line in TS was deleted here by WSB: "(Of course in this film Clem turns out to be a heroic undercover CIA agent.)"

61. NYPLTS 1 has the word "INSERT" written in WSB's hand, but there is no text present to insert.

62. Mao Zedong or Mao Tse-tung, 1893–1976, founder of the People's Republic of China and China's leader from 1949 until his death.

63. Greek junta: a military junta that ruled Greece from 1967 to 1974 and was widely criticized for its brutal tactics.

64. "too rapid" is a WSB holographic insert in NYPLTS 1.

65. WSB spelling.

66. Land of Mu: a fictional lost continent proposed by Augustus Le Plongeon in the 19th century.

67. "virgin" is a WSB holographic insert in NYPLTS 1.

68. WSB spelling for "tributaries."

69. "vun" changed from "one" per WSB tape; "German" accent used throughout this passage.

70. Graham Greene, *The Heart of the Matter* (Portsmouth, NH: Heinemann, 1948).

71. WSB changed "bowel" to "foul" in holographic change in NYPLTS 1; on the tape, it could be either "bowel" or "foul."

72. NYPLTS 1 has "for" crossed out, substituted by "where" on WSB tape.

73. *Night of the Living Dead*, 1968, classic zombie movie directed by George A. Romero.

74. WSB spelling of "analgesics."

75. NYPLTS 1 has WSB holographic insert here of the word "even."

76. NYPLTS 1 has "You mean that" crossed out before the word "capture."

77. NYPLTS 1 has "Exactly." crossed out here.

78. Dumheits: *Dummheiten* in German means "stupidities."

79. The following "MOB Statement" was inserted here in NYPLTS 1, with the following crossed-out header:

> SIGMA PORTFOLIO : SIGMA PORTFOLIO :
> SIGMA PORTFOLIO : MOB s.p.no. 37
> The original Mob statement will form the
> editorial of the first number of the tabloid
> —for this we are indebted to William Burroughs

The insert ends with the phrase ". . . any more than a small pox virus." (page 33).

80. Charles Manson (1934–2017) formed the Manson Family in California in the 1960s. He was convicted of the murder of Sharon Tate and others.

81. "Weigh" in WSB NYPLTS 1.

82. *The Invisible Generation,* published in two parts in *International Times,* London, issue 3, 1966, and issue 6, 1967. The text of Invisible Generation was also published as a poster by *International Times* as issue 5.5 in December 1966. The poster used a fragment of Burroughs' text that could be cut out and assembled into a word scrambler.

83. AZTS 1 indicates a paragraph indentation at "BLOODY WEDNESDAY."

84. These cities were the locations of major demonstrations, riots, and suppressive police actions in 1968 and 1970: Chicago at the Democratic Convention August 1968; Paris in May 1968; the huge massacre of students and others in Tlatelolco (Mexico) in October 1968; and the killings of students at Kent State University in Ohio, May 1970.

85. AZTS 1 gas "the demonstrators."

86. AZTS 1 has "lines."

87. AZTS 1 has no quotation marks around this sentence.

88. James Callaghan, 1912–2005, Chancellor of the Exchequer, Home Secretary, Foreign Secretary, and Prime Minister of the United Kingdom (not simultaneously), 1964–79.

89. AZTS 1 has no quotation marks around this sentence.

90. AZTS 1 has "magazine."

91. Trân Lệ Xuân, 1924–2011, popularly known as Madame Nhu, was the de facto First Lady of Vietnam, 1955–63.

92. Hendrik Verwoerd, Prime Minister of South Africa, 1958–66, when he was assassinated; he was one of the primary developers of apartheid.

93. AZTS 1 has "scramble" as holographic edit of typed "scandal."

94. The Voice of America is the official radio and TV broadcast agency of the U.S. government.

95. In Vale MS as "Fatima"; a common woman's name used here to indicate a servant.

96. A long insert follows from WSB's *Electronic Revolution* [ER] (Cambridge: Henri Chopin, 1971).

97. Richard C. French, "Electronic Arts of Noncommunication," *New Scientist* 47 (June 4, 1970): 470. WSB also gives an incorrect date of July 2 for this article in other references to it. WSB edits and/or paraphrases the passages from French's article somewhat.

98. Ian Sommerville, 1940–76, a computer programmer who worked with WSB and Brion Gysin on a number of book and cutup projects;

Antony Balch, 1937–80, a filmmaker who worked with WSB and Gysin on a number of film projects.

99. French's article has "0.05."

100. Dim-N: apparently a reference to N,N-Dimethyltryptamine, the active ingredient in Ayahuasca, a drug used by Amazonian shamans, which WSB had experimented with.

101. GPU: *Gosudarstvennoye politicheskoye upravlenie* (State Political Directorate under the NKVD of the RSFSR), an early (1922–23) Soviet secret police agency.

102. Probably a reference to the 1906 San Francisco earthquake; a cargo ship in Halifax exploded disastrously in 1917.

103. Phun City was an open-air rock festival organized by *International Times,* July 24–26, 1970, at Ecclesden Common, Worthing, Sussex. The planned sci-fi symposium on the 25th did not get off the ground. Burroughs was present, recording the crowd, and did a reading instead.

104. Passage from ER ends here. See Supplement 2, from AZTS 1, 2 leaves referring to speech scramblers.

105. AZTS 1 has "past" for "absent."

106. Dr. Har Gobind Khorana, 1922–2011, a biochemist who, along with Marshall W. Nirenberg and Robert W. Holley, received the 1968 Nobel Prize for Physiology or Medicine for work involving studies of genetic codes.

107. What follows paraphrases French's article (op cit., n97) and is an insert from ER; AZTS 1 indicates a paragraph should start here.

108. Daedalus: In Greek mythology, he was a great craftsman and artist and had much esoteric and sometimes dangerous knowledge. He is also the father of Icarus and made the wings Icarus used to fly too close to the sun.

109. Insert from ER ends here.

110. From here through the next few pages to the phrase ". . . only research can give is the answers," AZTS 1 has a number of minor differences of vocabulary from the tape; that entire passage has been transcribed in Supplement 4.

111. Wilson Smith, ed., *Mechanisms of Virus Infection* (London/New York: Academic Press, 1963).

112. AZTS 1 has a shorter quotation.

113. "Mr. Hart": The Unspeakable Mr. Hart, a WSB character, that appeared first in a comic strip and then in his book *Ah Pook Is Here.* QV. note 57 above.

114. Insert from ER begins here.

115. Insert from ER ends here.

116. AZTS 1 has minor differences of vocabulary and punctuation from the tape in this paragraph. To summarize: AZTS 1 has "here is" for "here's"; "its sure" for "let's show"; "rope" for "to rope"; "rumbles" for "grumblings"; "To do everything" for "*To do everything*";

"To do nothing" for "*To do nothing*"; "jumps up" for "he jumps up"; "a chair" for "the chair"; "can" for "could"; "and" for "or."

117. Insert from ER begins here.

118. ETC: very likely "etcetera" but also possibly a garbled reference to a drug.

119. "The Sunny Side of the Street": a popular song from the 1930s.

120. "hallucinogen."

121. Perhaps a reference to the Maya Celestial Bird god, Vucub Caquix, who was defeated in Xibalba (the underworld) by the hero twins Hunahpu and Xbalanque.

122. This passage seems to conflate the history and mythology of the Maya and the Aztecs. The "White God" would seem to refer to the arrival of the Spaniards, which some Aztecs at first thought might be the return of the culture hero Quetzalcoatl.

123. A quote, perhaps, from an unknown source, suggesting words from a Maya priest referring to the Maya calendar system.

124. There are many forms of a Young Maize God in Maya and Meso-american culture generally. One of his most well-known forms today is as Hun Hunahpu, the father of Hunahpu and Xbalanque, as recounted in the Quiché book *Popol Vuh*.

125. Diego de Landa, 1524–79, Bishop of Yucatán. He was responsible for the burning of many of the Maya codices (three are known to have survived) and was ruthless in trying to convert the Maya to Roman Catholicism. But he also wrote *Relación de las cosas de Yucatán,* a major source of information about pre-Columbian Maya culture.

126. Since WSB wrote this, there have been enormous strides in reading Maya writing and epigraphy, in the remaining books, on ceramics, and on stone sculpture and stelae. Much of it has now been transcribed and interpreted.

127. Insert from ER ends here.

128. The preceding paragraph has several minor differences from the tape: AZTS 1 has "this" for "thus"; "speak" for "talk"; "I have" for "I've"; "multi-level" for "multi-leveled"; "with a" for "to the"; "I" for "and"; "the" for "their."

129. Alfred Habdank Skarbek Korzybski, 1879–1950, Polish American philosopher and scientist who developed an important theory of general semantics, in which human thought and perception are influenced by the structure of language. In WSB's *The Book of Breeething* (Ohio University Press, 1974), there is the following passage referring to Korzybski's ideas: "Count Alfred Korzybski, who developed the concept of General Semantics in his book *Science and Sanity,* has pointed out that the is of identity has led to basic confusion in Western thought. The is of identity is rarely used in Egyptian pictorial writing. Instead of saying he is my servant they say he (is omitted) *as* my servant: a statement of relationship not identity. Accordingly

there is nothing that word itself essentially *is*. Word only exists in a communication system of sender and receiver. It takes two to talk. Perhaps it only took one to write" (quoted from the 1979 edition in *Ah Pook Is Here and Other Texts,* op cit.)

130. AZTS 1 has "verb"; tape has "word." We have adopted the AZTS 1 reading here.

131. AZTS 1 has "*and.*"

132. AZTS 1 has "customs and passport."

133. AZTS 1 has "Definite article . . ."; not "The definite article. . . ."

134. AZTS 1 has "body" for "virus."

135. The two lines "Keep the home fires burning / Though ["While" in the actual lyrics] the hearts are yearning" are from a popular song of the World War I; "There's a long, long trail awinding . . ." is from a different World War I popular song.

136. Line from the Civil War anthem "The Battle Hymn of the Republic."

137. WSB says "Mass Association" on WSB tape.

# ABOUT THE EDITORS AND CONTRIBUTORS

GEOFFREY D. SMITH is Professor Emeritus, former head of the Rare Books and Manuscripts Library of The Ohio State University Libraries, and adjunct professor in the Department of English. He was also longtime steward of the William S. Burroughs Collection at Ohio State. His PhD is in American Literature and Textual Studies from Indiana University.

JOHN M. BENNETT is the founding curator of the Avant Writing Collection at The Ohio State University Libraries. He was editor of the international literary journal *Lost and Found Times* from 1975 to 2005 and is the publisher of Luna Bisonte Prods, promoting avant literatures since 1974. His PhD is in Latin American Literature from UCLA.

ANTONIO BONOME is a visual artist, scholar, and philologist studying William S. Burroughs' work as a process-based art form.

V. VALE is a counterculture writer and publisher and the sole proprietor/founder of RE/Search Publications. He published part of Burroughs' "The Revised Boy Scout Manual" in 1982 in *RE/Search #4/5: William S. Burroughs, Brion Gysin, and Throbbing Gristle*.